APPROACHES IN CURRICULUM

Prentice-Hall Viewpoints and Alternatives Series
Ronald T. Hyman,
Consulting Editor

APPROACHES IN CURRICULUM
   Ronald T. Hyman
EARLY CHILDHOOD EDUCATION
   Bernard Spodek

Edited by
Ronald T. Hyman
Rutgers University

APPROACHES IN CURRICULUM

Prentice-Hall, Inc., Englewood Cliffs, New Jersey

Library of Congress Cataloging in Publication Data

HYMAN, RONALD T   comp.
    Approaches in curriculum.

    (Prentice-Hall viewpoints and alternatives series)
    CONTENTS: Dewey, J. The subject-matter of
education.—Kilpatrick, W. H. The essentials of the
activity movement.—Stratemeyer, F. Developing a
curriculum for modern living.—Hand, H. C. The case
for the common learnings course. [etc.]
    1. Education—Curricula—Addresses, essays,
lectures.   I. Title.
LB1570.H95   375'.001   72–10129
ISBN 0–13–043703–4
ISBN 0–13–043695–X (pbk)

© 1973 by Prentice-Hall Inc.
Englewood Cliffs, New Jersey

10   9   8   7   6   5   4   3   2   1

Printed in the United States of America

PRENTICE-HALL INTERNATIONAL, INC., London
PRENTICE-HALL OF AUSTRALIA, PTY., INC., Sydney
PRENTICE-HALL OF CANADA, LTD., Toronto
PRENTICE-HALL OF INDIA PRIVATE LIMITED, New Delhi
PRENTICE-HALL OF JAPAN, INC., Tokyo

for ART RITTENBERG

CONTENTS

PART I

INTRODUCTION   *3*

PART II

SELECTED
CURRICULUM
ALTERNATIVES

1   THE SUBJECT-MATTER OF EDUCATION   *23*
John Dewey

A curriculum focus centering on the continuing reconstruction
of experience

**2   THE ESSENTIALS
OF THE ACTIVITY MOVEMENT   *29***
William Heard Kilpatrick

A curriculum focus centering on activities

**3   DEVELOPING A CURRICULUM
FOR MODERN LIVING**   *53*
Florence Stratemeyer

A curriculum focus centering on persistent life situations

**4   THE CASE FOR
THE COMMON LEARNINGS COURSE**   *73*
Harold C. Hand

The curriculum focus centering on common learnings

5   ENCOUNTER: A Theory of the Curriculum Which Affirms the
Centrality of the Communities of Discourse   *88*
Arthur R. King, Jr. and John A. Brownell

A curriculum focus centering on the structure of the separate
academic disciplines

6   WHAT KNOWLEDGE IS OF MOST WORTH?   *101*
Arno A. Bellack

A curriculum focus centering on broad fields, social problems,
and modes of thought

**7   INTEGRATIVE EDUCATION FOR
A DIS-INTEGRATED WORLD**   *121*
Gene Wise

A curriculum focus centering on existential integration

8   RELEVANCE AND THE CURRICULUM   *140*
Lawrence E. Metcalf and Maurice P. Hunt

A curriculum focus centering on youth's views of society

**9   HIGH SCHOOL STUDENT PROTEST AND
THE NEW CURRICULUM WORKER**   *153*
John S. Mann

A curriculum focus centering on student protest

10   **COMMUNICATION:** A Curriculum Focus   *178*
Margaret Ammons

A curriculum focus centering on a single process

11   **NEW CURRICULUM DESIGNS FOR CHILDREN**   *201*
Louise M. Berman

A curriculum focus centering on humanistic processes

PART IIII

SELECTED BIBLIOGRAPHY   *219*

CONTRIBUTORS

John Dewey
Columbia University

William Heard Kilpatrick
Teachers College, Columbia University

Florence Stratemeyer
Teachers College, Columbia University

Harold C. Hand
University of Illinois

Arthur R. King, Jr.
University of Hawaii

John A. Brownell
Claremont Graduate School

Arno A. Bellack
Teachers College, Columbia University

Gene Wise
Case Western Reserve University

Lawrence E. Metcalf
University of Illinois

Maurice P. Hunt
Fresno State College

John S. Mann
University of New Mexico

Margaret Ammons
University of Wisconsin

Louise M. Berman
University of Maryland

APPROACHES IN CURRICULUM

PART I

INTRODUCTION

part I
THE CURRICULUM ISSUE

The question, "What shall I teach?" poses itself to every teacher before and during the time he meets with his students. Curriculum essentially and primarily deals with this issue. No one teacher can teach everything nor can one student learn everything. Selection is therefore necessary. Even in areas of specialization, it is impossible to evade the curriculum question.

This problem is particularly acute when an elementary or secondary school faculty must provide an answer on a broad front.

Such a faculty is responsible by law for the schooling of the students during many hours of many days over many years because we do have compulsory school attendance. The teachers must choose what to teach and how to organize and emphasize the selected content. This focusing task is a basic one facing every teaching body.[1]

A focus is necessary to give coherence and rationality to the decisions made concerning the curriculum. Louise M. Berman puts it this way, "The curriculum must establish its points of emphasis or priority. Without such emphases the curriculum becomes bland and does not provide for means of dealing with problems of conflicting interests." [2] Even those teachers who do not explicitly set forth a curriculum focus demonstrate one through their actions. That is to say, a curriculum focus emerges as the outward manifestation of curriculum decisions. In some cases the focus may be less sharp as teachers fail to commit themselves to certain actions that would bring coherence and completeness to their curriculum.

The *subject matter** of the curriculum, or content, ought not to be confused with its focus for teaching purposes. It is possible for two different foci, for example, to both indicate to the teacher to teach that the Declaration of Independence serves as the foundation of the U.S. political structure. Both foci may direct students to learn that the U.S. government derives its "just powers from the consent of the governed." Yet one focus may organize this short quotation from the Declaration of Independence under the category of political science discipline and direct students to learn it as they study the key concepts of political science, whereas the second focus may organize it under the broad theme of World Peace and direct students to learn it as they seek answers to "Should the U.S. Ban the Hydrogen Bomb?"

---

* The term subject matter means the *knowledge* (i.e., facts, explanations, principles, definitions), *skills and processes* (i.e., reading, writing, calculating, dancing, critical thinking decision making, communicating), and *values* (i.e., the beliefs about matters concerned with good and bad, right and wrong, beautiful and ugly). Every society creates and uses its own unique subject matter. There are overlappings in subject matter from one society to the next. It is from a society's subject matter that a teacher selects.[3]

In this way the selected subject matter becomes related both in time and concept to various other bits of knowledge, skills, and values. Because of this, the importance and meaning of the selected subject matter changes depending on the curriculum focus. That is, the context for teaching subject matter significantly influences the meaning and value of it.

For this reason the curriculum question is not merely one of selecting subject matter. Since there is much subject matter to deal with even after selection, the teacher must simultaneously select, organize, and direct. These three tasks are so interrelated that each one influences the other two.

A curriculum focus is an emphasis and direction for the selected content. It establishes how the selected items will be related to each other in concept and in time. It influences the determination of the method of teaching and the placement of students with teachers. A curriculum focus is the combination of direction (purpose), selection, and organization of subject matter, and, in deciding upon one, a person brings into perspective other curricular decisions, such as who will teach whom, how to teach, how to organize the teachers and students into groups, when to teach what, and how to evaluate the curriculum, teachers, and students.

Because various teachers, or groups of teachers, have their own perspectives from which to view the subject matter of a society, they will have different curriculum direction. For this reason a curriculum is a "reflection of what people think, feel, believe, and do." [4] The determination of a focus is also obviously influenced by the critical events of the times and thus there is a time and location setting within which each curriculum takes shape.

It is precisely with these alternative curriculums that this book is concerned. Today's curriculum worker can operate wisely only if he is aware of alternatives. He cannot act reasonably if he assumes that his current focus is and must be the only one chosen, or if he is ignorant of other people's formulations. To know the various alternatives available—allowing for adaptations due to time and location—is to permit and encourage sensible curriculum decision making.

The Current Overall Approach to
Curriculum Development

People who teach hold a fundamental belief that they can and do effect changes in their students, that teaching results in change. (Whether these changes are desirable changes in *overt* behavior or in some *predisposition* to change overt behavior is still an open matter.) Teachers cannot hold that teaching is futile, that the student is beyond help or incapable of learning.

On this basis teachers set forth the changes they seek to effect and then establish the curriculum focus they think will bring about those changes. That is to say, they establish their goals (objectives) and then establish the curriculum to attain them; they set their ends and determine the means to reach them.

This is a common approach in our society. Statesmen set their ends and then determine the legislation and enforcement procedures needed to achieve their policies. Doctors, generals, engineers, carpenters, and many others follow a similar pattern. In regard to curriculum work we can trace the use of this common approach back centuries, but it emerged as a recognized, professional idea at the beginning of the twentieth century.[5] Early curriculum practitioners such as Franklin Bobbitt and W. W. Charters accepted and employed this approach unquestioningly.

This means-ends approach to curriculum work appears most clearly when educators: 1. establish objectives as intended outcomes to be reached, 2. determine a curriculum focus and a teaching method, 3. organize the teachers and pupils, and 4. evaluate their activities to see if they reached their objectives. This step-by-step approach to curriculum development is most commonly disseminated through the work and writing of Ralph Tyler, a disciple of Bobbitt and Charters. The "Tyler rationale" was set forth in his now classic syllabus for Education 360 at the University of Chicago, *Basic Principles of Curriculum and Instruction*. Tyler wrote his book as an attempt "to explain a rationale for viewing, analyzing, and interpreting the curriculum and instruction program of an educational institution. . . . This book outlines one way of viewing an institutional program as a functioning instrument of education." [6]

The Tyler rationale centers around "four fundamental questions which must be answered in developing any curriculum and plan of instruction. These are:

1. What educational purposes should the school seek to attain?
2. What educational experiences can be provided that are likely to attain these purposes?
3. How can these educational experiences be effectively organized?
4. How can we determine whether these purposes are being attained?" [7]

It is important to note that these questions are to be answered in the order asked. For this reason the stating of objectives is the crucial step for Tyler since the other three responses are given in light of the objectives chosen. Tyler puts this point about objectives succinctly and clearly at the beginning of his book: "These educational objectives become the criteria by which materials are selected, content is outlined, instructional procedures are developed, and tests and examinations are prepared. All aspects of the educational program are really means to accomplish basic educational purposes. Hence, if we are to study an educational program systematically and intelligently we must first be sure as to the educational objectives aimed at." [8]

Though Tyler himself indicates that his rationale is but one way of viewing curriculum matters (see the first quotation from Tyler), the Tyler formulation has crystallized to become *the* rationale. Many students even fail to realize that there can be other rationales. This failure is due to the inaccessibility of other rationales and the lack of curriculums developed according to them. Many students also fail to realize that curriculum development according to a step-by-step approach began before 1949, the year Tyler first published his syllabus. The case is, rather, that Tyler in 1949 just formally presented his interpretation of an approach that had been utilized for at least thirty years by curriculum theorists and practitioners. We have, then, in the Tyler rationale only one man's formulation of one approach to curriculum development, but one that has risen to the position of near dogma.

Recently there have appeared some published doubts, questions, and criticisms of the value and use of the Tyler rationale and, in particular, the primacy of objectives. For example, there arises the valid point that the stating of objectives in specific and simple behavioral terms (as advocated by the Tyler people) does indeed restrict the curriculum. Their specificity can limit teachers who are generally interested in broad changes so as to maintain curricular flexibility. Moreover, teachers are not interested merely in changing behavior that is overt, observable, and measurable. Teaching, in contrast to brainwashing, threatening, and torturing, attempts to induce changes in thinking patterns, which are not observable or measurable, as well as changes in overt behavior, which are observable and, in some instances, measurable. To be concerned only with overt, measurable behavior is inadequate, but even if we were concerned only with this, it would still be inadequate to consider such behavior without considering the reasons behind it.[9]

What is important here is not whether the Tyler rationale is valid or invalid but that it is still the overall general framework in use today for curriculum design and, as such, should be presented along with some of the issues it raises. The literature criticizing the Tyler rationale and the factors constituting it is growing. The student of curriculum would do well to study and understand the arguments and counter-arguments as they affect the future work of curriculum design and the various proposals offered by curriculum workers.[9]

The Determination of a Curriculum Focus

The selection, organization, and direction of subject matter is an act of great importance not only to the teacher and his students but also to the public at large and because of this, the decisions arrived at need to be made in some rational, acceptable way. Without a rational approach confusion, chaos, and "noncoordination" of efforts set in to bedevil the teaching situation. Scheffler begins his article on "Justifying Curriculum Decisions" with this idea in mind when he says:

> Decisions that confront educators are notoriously varied, complex, and far-reaching in importance, but none outweighs in difficulty or significance those decisions governing selection of content. . . .
> We do not . . . consider it a matter of indifference or whim just what the educator chooses to teach. Some selections we judge better than others; some we deem positively intolerable. Nor are we content to discuss issues of selection as if they hinged on personal taste alone. We try to convince others; we present ordered arguments; we appeal to custom and principle; we point to relevant consequences and implicit commitments. In short, we consider decisions on educational content to be responsible or justifiable acts with public significance.[10]

We justify curriculum decisions by appealing to criteria. Criteria are standards that we use to help us in making valid decisions. To show that a decision is acceptable we show that it conforms to established criteria. Criteria for selection, organization and direction are, therefore, crucial for teachers.

Criteria* also serve to widen our range of decisions and to alert us to having possibly slighted certain material. They are "needed for assurance that temporary needs and feelings of urgency will not overwhelm other basic functions of education, that omissions will be considered as carefully as additions, and that in the course of establishing priorities of time spent, the possibilities of

---

* Criteria are not the same as objectives with which they are sometimes confused. Criteria are used when several alternative items are available to attain an objective, an intended outcome. We use the criteria to decide which of the alternative items are preferable. Indeed, there are many alternatives available in curriculum matters that can lead to commonly stated objectives.

increased efficiency in learning and teaching will not be over-looked." [11]

Curriculum workers must also establish the criteria they will follow. They can accept a set of criteria proposed by someone else, formulate their own criteria independently, or accept parts of various sets of criteria combined with their own formulations.

Two sets of criteria are presented below. They are illustrative of the many available in the literature. These two will suffice to further alert the reader to the importance of criteria, to give him a basis for formulating his own set if he so chooses, and to offer a good starting point for examining alternative foci.

A. Criteria Proposed by Taba[12]

1. Curriculum content is valid and significant to the extent that it reflects the contemporary scientific knowledge. . . . But perhaps the more important question about validity of content is how fundamental the knowledge is. . . .

2. If the curriculum is to be a useful prescription for learning, its content and the outcomes it pursues need to be in tune with the social and cultural realities of the time. Applied to the selection of content, this criterion further selects from the scientifically valid and fundamental knowledge that which is also significant. . . .

3. Curriculum should represent an appropriate balance of breadth and depth. . . .

4. Curriculum should provide for the achievement of a wide range of objectives. An effective curriculum provides for acquisition of significant new knowledge *and* for the development of increasingly more effective ways of thinking, desirable attitudes and interests, and appropriate habits and skills. . . .

5. Curriculum content should be learnable and adaptable to students' experiences. . . . One factor in learnability is the adjustment of the curriculum content and of the focus of learning experiences to the abilities of the learners. . . . The problem of making the curriculum learn-

able involves also the task of translating the social heritage into experiences which help each student to make it his own. . . .

6. The curriculum should be appropriate to the needs and interests of the learners.

B. Criteria Proposed by Scheffler[13]

"The guiding principle underlying the following rules is that educational content is to help the learner attain maximum self-sufficiency as economically as possible."

1. Presumably, self-sufficiency can be brought about economically or extravagantly; content should be selected that is judged most economical. Three types of economy are relevant. First, content should be economical of teaching effort and resources. Second, content should be economical of learners' effort. . . . Finally, we must consider economy of subject matter; content should have maximum generalizability or transfer value. The notion of generalizability is, however, ambiguous. Accordingly, two types of subject-matter economy need to be distinguished. First, is there an empirically ascertainable tendency for the learning of some content to facilitate other learning? Presumably, this sort of question was at issue in the controversy over classics and it was discussed in terms of empirical studies. Second, is the content sufficiently central logically to apply to a wide range of problems? This is not a psychological question but one that concerns the structure of available knowledge. Nevertheless, it is through some such principle of economy, in the logical sense that we decide to teach physics rather than meteorology, for instance, where other considerations are balanced. . . .

2. Content should enable the learner to make responsible personal and moral decisions. Self-awareness, imaginative weighing of alternative courses of action, understanding of other people's choices and ways of life, decisiveness without rigidity, emancipation from stereotyped ways of thinking and perceiving—all these are

bound up with the goal of personal and moral self-sufficiency. . . .

3. Since personal and moral decisions are not made in a vacuum, their execution requires technical skills of various sorts. Content should thus provide students with the technical or instrumental prerequisites for carrying out their decisions. What this goal may require in practice will vary from situation to situation; but, speaking generally, mathematics, languages, and the sciences are, I believe, indispensible subjects, while critical ability, personal security and independent power of judgment in the light of evidence are traits of instrumental value in the pursuit of any ends. . . .

4. Finally, beyond the power to make and to carry out decisions, self-sufficiency requires intellectual power. Content, that is, should provide theoretical sophistication to whatever degree possible. Here we may distinguish between logical, linguistic, and critical proficiency—the ability to formulate and appraise arguments in various domains, on the one hand, and acquaintance with basic information as well as with different modes of experience and perception, on the other.

Hilda Taba and Gail Inlow, curriculum specialists, have made significant points about criteria in their writings on the selection of subject matter. These points deserve the reader's attention because of the centrality of criteria in the curriculum question. In combination they restate the value and function of criteria as well as the procedure for using them.

Finally, it is evident that whatever the criteria, they need to be applied as a collective set of screens through which to sift the possibilities in order to assure that only experiences that are valid in the light of all pertinent considerations find their way into the curriculum. An exclusive use of any one criterion or of a limited set of criteria involves a danger of an unbalanced curriculum. To produce an effective as well as efficient curriculum it is necessary to retain only that content and those learning experiences which survive the sifting process after the application of all relevant criteria of a good curriculum.[14]

These and related criteria serve education's diagnostic purposes as the x-ray serves medicine. Individually and collectively, criteria permit professional curriculum personnel to penetrate into the vitals of curriculum substance and related practices to the end of detecting and setting apart the pathological from the healthy. Although no criterion constellation is infallible, any one that is reasonably thought out cannot help purifying, at least in part, the process of curriculum development or curriculum change. The schools that refuse to look at themselves in some approved systematized way invariably are schools that offer the same content year after year, and make the same mistakes year after year. Society's current mood may not be one to condone, for very long, such indifference and sloth.[15]

With his set of criteria—either explicitly worked out or implicitly held in mind—the teacher establishes his curriculum focus. As he formulates a curriculum focus to propose to others for acceptance, the teacher manifests his objectives and criteria, he cannot do otherwise. Thus the curriculum focus is the outward manifestation of many curriculum decisions. The astute analyst of a curriculum focus is able to infer from it the objectives and criteria held by the proposer even if they are not set forth explicitly. An examination of a curriculum focus is a sure way to discover just what beliefs a teacher holds about curriculum matters.

With this point in mind we turn to the proposed alternative curriculum foci.

part II
OVERVIEW OF THE SELECTED CURRICULUM FOCI

A. The Need for Alternatives

A teacher may speak favorably about his own classroom or his own individual school. But the overall feeling today in America is that there is serious trouble in our schools. Criticism abounds. One classroom teacher oriented magazine, *Media and Methods*,[16] summarized its mail from students commenting on the schools with the simple, short, trenchant sentence, "School is a bore." Adult critics agree with the students and call for reforming the schools by creating alternatives—alternative approaches within the established school system as well as alternative school systems.[17] The key word is "alternatives."

In either case, reform of the established school system or reform through the establishment of an alternative school system, curriculum workers need to work on alternative curriculum foci if they are to fulfill the country's call for a change in the essence of schooling. The heart of schooling is the curriculum and it must be changed if any other changes are to be of value.

A curriculum worker needs to be alert to and knowledgeable about alternative curriculum proposals. He must know just what is the case for each of the available alternatives. For example, what is the case for a curriculum focus centering on the academic disciplines? What is the case for a curriculum focus centering on persistent life situations? On the needs and interests of students? On processes?

Only when the teacher is knowledgeable and aware, can he wisely work for change. With the curriculum worker, as with any professional, intelligent action can occur *only when alternatives are possible and known.* That curriculum alternatives are *possible* is a realization that teachers and the public come to upon a few minutes' reflection. The treatment of the means-ends approach to curriculum development in the previous pages demonstrates this realization, too. So that the teacher can *know* some of the possible alternatives, the following selected articles appear.

B. A Perspective for Reading These Representative Proposals

The selections in this book are offered as representative of the several fundamental positions in curriculum that have evolved. That is to say, people criticizing today's curriculum and proposing curriculum alternatives take positions similar to some previously taken ones. By carefully examining these positions the reader learns about past proposals and also prepares himself for understanding current and future ones. Knowledge of these representative proposals can help the reader when he encounters new proposals since he will readily identify key elements in them.

Professor Alice Miel has examined past curriculum proposals to see if there is a pattern of development. She recognizes that proposals that have been neglected for a time return to attract renewed attention. To describe the pattern she found, Miel uses a model of an ascending spiral which enlarges as it climbs. (See Figure 1.) For her the spiral "accounts for the fact that proposals made at a later point in educational history usually are much more refined with wisdom distilled from experience at both sides of the spiral built into them. At each new point on the upward and outward spiral

FIGURE 1

Reprinted with the permission of the publisher from Dwayne Huebner's *A Reassessment of the Curriculum* (New York: Teachers College Press), c. 1964. p. 16.

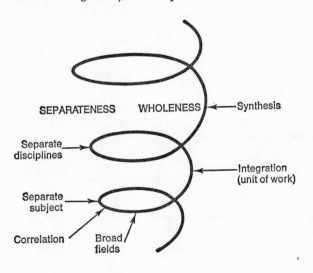

the concepts are clearer and the language of education is more precise." [18]

Miel applies her spiral model by plotting each decade in the twentieth century according to its chief characteristic. Her spiral time line is shown in Figure 2. The reader might well consider the spiral model both as an introduction to the selected articles here and as a springboard for a concluding reaction to them. But whether or not the reader wishes to accept Miel's spiral as the appropriate pictorial model for viewing curriculum proposals, there is little doubt that basic proposals are renewed periodically, sometimes gaining and holding public attention, sometimes not.

The authors of the selections offered in this book propose alternative curriculum foci for the reader to consider. These articles deliberately range in date of original publication from the turn of

FIGURE 2

Reprinted with the permission of the publisher from Dwayne Huebner's *A Reassessment of the Curriculum* (New York: Teachers College Press), c. 1964. p. 20.

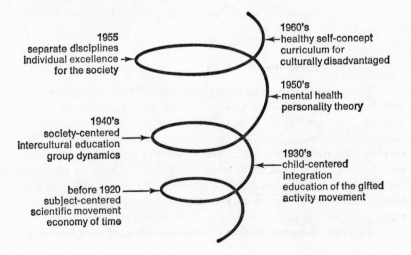

this century through the 1970's and as such offer concrete examples of the history of curriculum thought. More importantly, these articles take a stand. Each strives, in a forceful and lively style, to present the case for its particular curriculum focus. The reader might well retitle each article on his own as "The Case for —————" by filling in the blank appropriately. Indeed, the article by Harold Hand does just that already, being called, "The Case for the Common Learnings Course."

Because of their strong advocating style, these selections require the keen, critical attention of the reader. The reader must assess each case presented. Some key questions he might ask to guide himself are:

1. Is the case for this particular curriculum focus cogent and convincing? (In answering, the reader should examine the author's criteria used in justifying his decisions.)
2. What are the probable consequences of implementing this curriculum focus in our schools?
3. Is this proposal acceptable today for a wide range of schools, teachers, and students?
4. To what extent does this proposal agree with the Tyler rationale and/or modify it in light of the criticisms about it?

C. Categorizing the Selections

In his short book *The Child and the Curriculum* written in 1902 John Dewey identified two "sects" that emerged in curriculum matters. One sect "fixes its attention upon the importance of the subject-matter of the curriculum" and the other sect considers the child as "the starting-point, the center, and the end" of the curriculum.[19] Dewey then went on to show his opposition to both of these "oppositions." In spite of his own position, Dewey offered (via his identification of the two sects) a simple way of grouping alternative curriculum foci, at least at the turn of the century.[20]

Through the years so many variations of these two opposing

sects have appeared that Dewey's early classification scheme no longer appears to work neatly. It does not work well for those curriculum foci that come between the two extremes by borrowing something from each side and blending it in a unique way. Dewey himself realized that in practice the opposing extremes rarely occur. He wrote, "Such oppositions are rarely carried to their logical conclusion. Common-sense recoils at the extreme character of these results. They are left to theorists, while common-sense vibrates back and forward in a maze of inconsistent compromise." [21]

For this reason it is difficult to classify neatly, or even to label accurately each proposal. Nor is it possible to completely separate the foci from each other since they have obvious elements in common. The teacher who looks for a clean separation of curriculum foci into discrete categories looks in vain. It is in this light that the following labeling suggestions are made and used in this book in presenting these selected curriculum alternatives:

A Curriculum Focus Centering on:
1. The Continuing Reconstruction of Experience (Dewey)
2. Activities (Kilpatrick)
3. Persistent Life Situations (Stratemeyer)
4. Common Learnings (Hand)
5. The Structure of the Separate Academic Disciplines (King & Brownell)
6. Broad Fields, Social Problems, and Modes of Thought (Bellack)
7. Existential Integration (Wise)
8. Youth's Views of the World (Metcalf & Hunt)
9. Student Protest (Mann)
10. A Single Process: Communication (Ammons)
11. Humanistic Processes (Berman)

REFERENCES

1. JOHN DEWEY, *Experience and Education* (New York: The Macmillan Company, 1938), p. 96.
2. LOUISE M. BERMAN, *New Priorities in the Curriculum* (Columbus, Ohio: Charles E. Merrill Publishing Co. 1968), p. 2.
3. B. OTHANEL SMITH, WILLIAM O. STANLEY, and J. HARLAN SHORES, *Fundamentals of Curriculum Development* (Yonkers-On-Hudson; World Book Co., 1957), p. 127.
4. SMITH, STANLEY, SHORES, p. 3.
5. HERBERT M. KLIEBARD, "The Curriculum Field in Retrospect," in *Technology and the Curriculum*, ed. Paul W. F. Witt (New York: Teachers College Press, 1968), pp. 69–84.
6. RALPH W. TYLER, *Basic Principles of Curriculum and Instruction* (Chicago: University of Chicago Press, 1949), p. 1.
7. TYLER, p. 1.
8. TYLER, p. 3.
9. See my own article "Means-Ends Reasoning and the Curriculum," *Teachers College Record* 73, No. 3 (February, 1972): 393–401 and the many references listed there on this point.
10. ISRAEL SCHEFFLER, "Justifying Curriculum Decisions," *School Review* 66, No. 4 (Winter, 1958): 461.
11. HILDA TABA, *Curriculum Development* (New York: Harcourt Brace Jovanovich, Inc., 1962), p. 265.
12. TABA, pp. 267–84.
13. SCHEFFLER, pp. 469–72.
14. TABA, p. 267.
15. GAIL INLOW, *The Emergent in Curriculum* (New York: John Wiley & Sons, Inc., 1966), p. 27.
16. *Media and Methods* 5, No. 8 (April, 1969).
17. See CHARLES SILBERMAN, *Crisis in the Classroom* (New York: Random House, Inc., 1970) and the many individual authors anthologized in *Radical School Reform*, ed. Beatrice and Ronald Gross (New York:

Simon & Schuster, Inc., 1969) and in *The Experience of Schooling*, ed. Melvin L. Silberman (New York: Holt, Rinehart and Winston, Inc., 1971).

18. ALICE MIEL, "Reassessment of the Curriculum—Why?" in *A Reassessment of the Curriculum*, ed. Dwayne Huebner (New York: Bureau of Publications, Teachers College, Columbia University, 1964), pp. 9–23.

19. JOHN DEWEY, *The Child and the Curriculum* in *Dewey on Education*, ed. Martin S. Dworkin (New York: Bureau of Publications, Teachers College, Columbia University, 1959), pp. 94–95.

20. See also the similar points by HUGH C. BLACK, "A Four Fold Classification of Educational Theories," *Educational Theory* 16, No. 3 (July, 1966): 281–91 and Arno A. Bellack, "Selection and Organization of Curriculum Content: An Analysis," in *What Shall the High Schools Teach?* ed. Arno A. Bellack, 1956 Yearbook (Washington: D.C., Association for Supervision and Curriculum Development, 1956), pp. 97–126.

21. DEWEY, *The Child and the Curriculum*, p. 96.

SELECTED CURRICULUM ALTERNATIVES

THE SUBJECT-MATTER
OF EDUCATION

JOHN DEWEY

This selection by John Dewey is Article III of his piece **My Pedagogic Creed** originally published in 1897. In its short, snappy, personal
style it gives the basis of the ideas Dewey used in establishing his
laboratory school at the University of Chicago in 1896. This is not
Dewey's most elaborate or mature proposal for a curriculum. It is,
however, the early foundation of his later works and as such most
significant.

The ideas proposed by Dewey as set forth in **Experience and
Education*** and **The Dewey School,**† two much later works, derive di-

---

* John Dewey, *Experience and Education* (New York: Macmillan, 1938).

† John Dewey, "The Theory of the Chicago Experiment," in *The Dewey*

rectly from this piece. For example, in 1897 in the selection reprinted here he says that "the subject-matter of the school curriculum should mark a gradual differentiation out of the primitive unconscious unity of social life" and that "education must be conceived as a continuing reconstruction of experience." Then in 1938 Dewey says that "finding the material for learning within experience is only the first step. The next step is the progressive development of what is already experienced into a fuller and richer and also more organized form, a form that gradually approximates that in which subject-matter is presented to the skilled, mature person." * Forty-one years after writing **My Pedagogic Creed** he still advocated the "continuous process of reconstruction of experience."

Though Dewey grew in stature as an educator and philosopher throughout his career at the University of Chicago and then Columbia University, he maintained the essence of his ideas on curriculum advocated here. His own response to the two curricular sects† the identifies is set forth clearly and fervently as a call to reform. The influence of the ideas contained in this selection is reflected in the reform movement of the first three decades of this century. The influence can be found easily in several other selections in this book but especially in the article by Kilpatrick (Chapter 2), Dewey's leading disciple, and Mann (Chapter 9) who specifically acknowledges Dewey. It is for these reasons that this early piece by Dewey is reprinted here.

◇◇◇

School by Katherine Camp Mayhew and Anna Camp Edwards (New York: Appleton-Century-Crofts, 1936). The book itself is an account of Dewey's Laboratory School at the University of Chicago, 1896–1903 by two sisters who worked at the school. The section by Dewey himself appears as an appendix in the book.

   * John Dewey, *Experience and Education*, p. 87.
   † See page 17 of the editor's Introduction to this book.

I believe that the social life of the child is the basis of concentration, or correlation, in all his training or growth. The social life gives the unconscious unity and the background of all his efforts and of all his attainments.

I believe that the subject-matter of the school curriculum should mark a gradual differentiation out of the primitive unconscious unity of social life.

I believe that we violate the child's nature and render difficult the best ethical results, by introducing the child too abruptly to a number of special studies, of reading, writing, geography, etc., out of relation to this social life.

I believe, therefore, that the true center of correlation on the school subjects is not science, nor literature, nor history, nor geography, but the child's own social activities.

I believe that education cannot be unified in the study of science, or so called nature study, because apart from human activity, nature itself is not a unity; nature in itself is a number of diverse objects in space and time, and to attempt to make it the center of work by itself, is to introduce a principle of radiation rather than one of concentration.

I believe that literature is the reflex expression and interpretation of social experience; that hence it must follow upon and not precede such experience. It, therefore, cannot be made the basis, although it may be made the summary of unification.

I believe once more that history is of educative value in so far as it presents phases of social life and growth. It must be controlled

"The Subject-Matter of Education" by John Dewey is reprinted from "My Pedagogic Creed," *The School Journal,* 54 (January 16, 1897): 77–80. This selection is Article III of the Creed.

by reference to social life. When taken simply as history it is thrown into the distant past and becomes dead and inert. Taken as the record of man's social life and progress it becomes full of meaning. I believe, however, that it cannot be so taken excepting as the child is also introduced directly into social life.

I believe accordingly that the primary basis of education is in the child's powers at work along the same general constructive lines as those which have brought civilization into being.

I believe that the only way to make the child conscious of his social heritage is to enable him to perform those fundamental types of activity which make civilization what it is.

I believe, therefore, in the so-called expressive or constructive activities as the center of correlation.

I believe that this gives the standard for the place of cooking, sewing, manual training, etc., in the school.

I believe that they are not special studies which are to be introduced over and above a lot of others in the way of relaxation or relief, or as additional accomplishments. I believe rather that they represent, as types, fundamental forms of social activity; and that it is possible and desirable that the child's introduction into the more formal subjects of the curriculum be through the medium of these activities.

I believe that the study of science is educational in so far as it brings out the materials and processes which make social life what it is.

I believe that one of the greatest difficulties in the present teaching of science is that the material is presented in purely objective form, or is treated as a new peculiar kind of experience which the child can add to that which he has already had. In reality, science is of value because it gives the ability to interpret and control the experience already had. It should be introduced, not as so much new subject-matter, but as showing the factors already involved in previous experience and as furnishing tools by which that experience can be more easily and effectively regulated.

I believe that at present we lose much of the value of literature and language studies because of our elimination of the social element. Language is almost always treated in the books of pedagogy simply as the expression of thought. It is true that language is a logical instrument, but it is fundamentally and primarily a social instrument. Language is the device for communication; it is the tool through which one individual comes to share the ideas and feelings of others. When treated simply as a way of getting individual information, or as a means of showing off what one has learned, it loses its social motive and end.

I believe that there is, therefore, no succession of studies in the ideal school curriculum. If education is life, all life has, from the outset, a scientific aspect, an aspect of art and culture, and an aspect of communication. It cannot, therefore, be true that the proper studies for one grade are mere reading and writing, and that at a later grade, reading, or literature, or science, may be introduced. The progress is not in the succession of studies but in the development of new attitudes towards, and new interests in, experience.

I believe finally, that education must be conceived as a continuing reconstruction of experience; that the process and the goal of education are one and the same thing.

I believe that to set up any end outside of education, as furnishing its goal and standard, is to deprive the educational process of much of its meaning and tends to make us rely upon false and external stimuli in dealing with the child.

2

THE ESSENTIALS OF
THE ACTIVITY MOVEMENT

WILLIAM HEARD KILPATRICK

During the three decades following World War I William Heard Kilpatrick, as Professor of Education at Teachers College, Columbia University, led the activity movement which grew out of the progressive thought advocated at the time. As the movement reached its peak, the National Society for the Study of Education (NSSE) devoted its 33rd Yearbook, Part II (1934) to a study of **The Activity Movement.** The **Yearbook** raised many "controverted points" and in this article Kilpatrick responds with a clear defense of the activity movement after briefly alluding to the NSSE **Yearbook.**

It is helpful here to specifically list some activities that curriculum thinkers considered at the time. In her book, **The Activity Concept,**

Lois Coffey Mossman provides a suggestive "listing of some of the enterprises in which learners of various ages may possibly engage." * (Kilpatrick himself wrote the warm and most supportive Introduction to Mossman's book.) Below are ten from her list of 76 activities:

1. Reading extensively and sharing interesting things to read, reading selections to the group, comparing interpretations.
2. Observing and recording data on bird activities and their nesting, and recording the time of arrival and of departure of migrating birds, and keeping lists of kinds of birds observed in a season.
3. Caring for pets, giving attention to suitable diets and living conditions.
4. Exploring history to find stories of ment who have met challenging situations or to find the beginnings of situations which are significant in life now.
5. Using part of the time of the individuals and of the group in participating in community enterprises and in furthering community living.
6. Conducting a class paper or participating in the conduct of a school or community paper.
7. Dramatizing interesting situations.
8. Writing stories and poems, composing music and dances, painting pictures, and modeling friezes.
9. Raising garden products and experimenting in growing plants.
10. Illustrating records and narratives of experiences.†

It is such activities that Kilpatrick has in mind and on which he wishes to focus the school's curriculum. It is through such activities that Kilpatrick wishes to develop the "whole child" and the "integration" of the student's personality since these activities embody the processes employed in living. On this point the reader should com-

---

* Lois Coffey Mossman, *The Activity Concept* (New York: The Macmillan Company, 1940), p. 61.

† Ibid., pp. 61–67.

pare Kilpatrick with Berman (Chapter 11), Ammons (Chapter 10), King and Brownell (Chapter 5), and Dewey (Chapter 1).

Finally, Kilpatrick briefly deals with the "based-on-physics view of life" and the "engineering" approach to education. Here the reader should refer back to the editor's section on the Tyler rationale treated in the Introduction to this book.

$\diamond$

It seems better in the opportunity here offered to discuss the heart of the problem rather than attempt seriatim answers on controverted points. One consistent view of the whole will possibly go farther at explaining than could any number of separate answers to disconnected objections and misunderstandings. Our task becomes then defined as the effort to find and state, as consistently as may be, the central doctrine or doctrines lying at the heart of the activity movement as this actually exists in this country.

The discussion herein attempted is difficult chiefly because of the opposed philosophies involved, though other differences further complicate the matter. The proponents and opponents of the activity movement, by the different ways in which they see the question in its ramifications, well illustrate the ambiguous gestalts which the psychology books discuss, those pictures which mean one thing from one view and quite another from a different viewpoint. Where the proponents of the movement see six cubes each clearly defined and all fitting well together, the opponents see seven cubes equally clear but different. The same facts confront, but the two groups see and organize them—and accordingly value them—in quite opposed fashion. Where the six-cube proponents see strength and promise, the seven-cube opponents see only confusion and danger.

The first and most obvious difference arises from the term "activity," as the constituent conception under review. The seven-cube opponents, themselves not using the term, go to the dictionary

"The Essentials of the Activity Movement" by William Heard Kilpatrick is reprinted from *Progressive Education* 11 (October, 1934): 346–59.

or to their knowledge of psychology and ask for the dictionary or the scientific definition of the word *activity*. They then conclude *deductively* what an "activity" ought to mean and so find confusion when the six-cube people using the term mean something else. One would have supposed that thinkers well used to scientific methods would in such case follow induction rather than deduction. It is quite interesting to find one critic speak slightingly of the inductive method of defining used in the *Yearbook,** calling it an "obvious expedient." One wonders what other method could be used under such circumstances. It should perhaps suffice to say that all dictionaries are made on the inductive basis; but we may further ask those who prefer to reason thus deductively about meaning to try their hands on such ordinary terms as "hogshead" and "Christian Science." Would the already known definitions of *hog* and *head,* or of *Christian* and *science* tell them what "hogshead" means as a measure of capacity, or "Christian Science" as a cult or movement? One does not have to be included among the adherents of the Christian Science faith to know that he must go to them to learn what the term means as they use it. Even if one wished to attack it, he must at least attack what it is.

Before taking up the more careful statement of the activity positions, let us make a preliminary comparison of the older, the traditional position, and that of the contrasting activity position.

The traditional position is essentially that of a curriculum composed of subject-matter-set-out-to-be-learned. (Some critics object to this compound term, but many proponents of the activity movement feel that it points with admirable precision to the essential difference between the two positions.) In accordance with this, *study* is essentially the effort to acquire what is thus set out; *learn* is its successful acquisition. The test of success is whether the learner can give back on demand what has thus been set out. The teacher must set the assignment, require its acquisition (peaceably, if he can; forcibly, if he must), then test the acquisition, and promote or fail

---

* *The Activity Movement,* 33rd Yearbook, Part II of the National Society for the Study of Education. See introduction to this article. R. T. H., ed.

accordingly. On this position, obvious pupil virtues are willingness to do as told, study hard, learn well, and recite accurately. Scientific (measuring) education, at its outset, accepted this general position. It sought to do these same things. The only difference was to do them better. While many present-day adherents have varied from the old spirit, this is in logic the original and clear-cut position.

Opposed to this we have a quite different position, as seen by those who most thoughtfully hold it. They wish the child to be more nearly self-directed, believing that only as he practices the best on his stage of intelligent self-direction can he learn to be more intelligently self-directing. That this may be possible, they further believe that the desirable school life should, in this respect, take on more of the quality of the best life outside of school. They therefore seek to have pupils engage in desirable purposeful activity, where the ends thus set up are the pupil's own and are felt and pursued as such. On this basis, *study* is the personal effort to deal intelligently with the situation at hand. Learning follows from study, but includes all resulting changes in the person (organism) as he thus works at the situation before him. Study and learning are now seen as inherent in the meaningful life process. What is learned is *not* set up in advance but accompanies and follows the efforts at meeting the situation, being called out by these efforts. "Subject-matter," if we still wish to use that term, includes on the study side all that one pays attention to or uses in the prosecution of the experience, and on the learning side all the learning results of all sorts. The school curriculum on this position does not consist of matter set-out-in-advance-to-be-learned, but of the succession of educative experiences so far as the school accepts responsibility for them. An "activity" thus means any distinguishable instance of such meaningful experience.

That there is, in this country and elsewhere, a movement which holds the essential position just set forth is beyond doubt. If objective evidence is demanded, one may refer to the various appendixes attached to the *Yearbook* or, just as well, open one's eyes to the educational world. In fact, Appendix 5 of the *Yearbook* raises the question whether some sixty per cent of the members of the National Society itself are not now ready to profess the position.

It may be well now to attempt a more definite statement of the theory underlying the activity movement. Some of the current emphases in biology offer a good start.

The very essence of life is the effort of the organism, whether human or of lower animal, to deal successfully with its confronting situation. The situation, *external or internal,* stirs the organism to action. The organism prefers one outcome rather than another, and it makes efforts accordingly. At the heart of this behavior process lies the fact of preference. Corresponding to efforts in behalf of preference are the facts of success or failure. Some theorists object to the use in this connection of such human-sounding terms as "preference," "effort," "success," and "failure." It is, of course, true that these terms reach their fullness of meaning only with the conscious life of men; but, even so, they seem needed to describe fittingly the actual facts of behavior wherever found. Stirring, preference, efforts, success or failure—these are ultimate conceptions for describing and explaining life.

Among the efforts in behalf of preference we must include that of *set.* To each defined stirring there arises (typically at any rate) a characteristic set of the organism as a whole, wherein it is made ready for the pursuit of the end implied in the stirring. This fact of set is easy to observe. A cat, for example, watching a bird to pounce on it has a clearly distinguishable set from that which it assumes when watching a dog that threatens danger. We need not see either bird or dog. The appearance of the cat suffices to tell us the character of the stirring that it feels. Every nerve and muscle, every pertinent resource of the cat's organism—even the very hairs—seem called out in coöperative readiness to act along the lines appropriate to success.

That the organism acts not by distinct parts but, in a true sense, as one whole—possibly in every act, certainly in many important acts—seems a fact established beyond doubt. Both the integrative action of the nervous system and the fact of set support the contention. The action of the endocrine glands add their substantiation, while such studies as Lashley's bring the facts of learning into conformity. The fact of set is but the obvious instance of organism working as a whole.

The fact that the organism thus acts as a whole has so many corollaries for education that one is tempted to delay the discussion in order to dwell on them. One instance definitely concerns us here. When the organism is stirred to vigorous action, should the first efforts fail, stronger efforts are put forth. If these fail, varying means are tried until success is attained or the available resources of the organism are exhausted. Be it noted that these persisting and varied efforts are not those of separate mechanisms, but of the organism acting as one unified whole. In such prolonged efforts it may well happen that the organism contrives a new response. This, if successful, is added to the organism's repertoire of resources and is so made available for future use.

A new response so contrived and so added to the resources of the organism is an instance of *learning*. Only living things learn. Clearly such learning involves both a creative aspect and a fixing aspect: the organism both contrives (creates) it and takes it on as an abiding addition to itself. An act of learning like this reaches far. It includes the organization into one response of many varied resources of the organism—nerve action, muscle action, feeling, thought, endocrine glands. So far as the body was stirred to share in the response, so far does the organized learning response extend. Any significant instance of learning, then, is a sort of cross-section of all that the organism was doing at the time, all welded into one whole. It is partly from such considerations that intelligent proponents of the activity movement reject the distinction and separation between mental and physical activity sought to be made by their opponents. The kind of activity which the proponents have in mind is as rich in content as all of life, but it all exists together without possibility of separation. Differences of degree from instance to instance, yes; separation of physical from mental, no. Such a separation would be as impossible as it is undesirable.

Besides the foregoing, there is another kind of learning. We used to call it "association." Nowadays, we often call it "conditioning." Even in the lower animals a sight or a sound or a smell may be so associated with an experience that its character as stimulus is completely changed. So a dog learns to come at a whistle, or cower at the threat of a whip. But this fact carries supreme possibilities. When an organism can respond not to the physical stimulus but to what it represents, then a new era lies at hand. Intelligence enters the world, meaning has appeared. For man, meanings constitute the raw material which, developed and organized, form what we call "mind." The original ability to get and use appropriate meanings we may call "innate intelligence." The resulting combined action of this innate ability and the organization of the meanings we have acquired, we may call one's "effectual intelligence." The aim and glory of education is to *increase* this effectual intelligence.

Experience in which we interact meaningfully with situations is thus the essence of human life. Being what we are, a situation stirs us chiefly by the meanings it arouses. We then react with efforts at controlling the situation according to our preferences. In these efforts we ourselves are progressively changed (i.e., we undergo learning effects) and we also change the situation. Study is the effort to deal intelligently with the situation at hand by bringing to bear on it the meaningful results of past experience. Study and learn are thus inherent in the very life process. Education is the cumulative result of such. In any instance of interaction with a situation, we give the name "environment" to all the elements in the situation to which the organism in any way reacts. Two persons might then be at substantially the same place at the same time and still have very different environments. As a person gains in knowledge and insight his actual environment increases. This is a crucial consideration as we deal with the young. In the degree that we succeed with our educative efforts, their environment grows in inclusiveness and in internal organization. To this end, they must learn ever better to react with effectual appropriateness. This process is the essence of social and moral education.

So far we have thought largely in biological terms. It becomes now necessary to inquire regarding the nature of the world we live in. The older educational view, which formed also the starting point for the scientific (measuring) movement, expected, as we have seen, to set before the young what they were to study and learn. This view began back in such days as Boas tells us about, when man could go thirty thousand years without perceptibly changing his culture.[1] In such days, and much later, each generation so nearly repeated the preceding that conscious education largely restricted itself to handing on to the rising generation what the elders had previously received from their parents.

Later, when knowledge began to be seriously studied, it was largely thought of as authoritatively fixed either by revelation or by necessary laws of nature and thought. In any case, it was the individual's duty to acquire and accept and act accordingly. Now this outlook implicitly supposed a fixed-in-advance future:

> Yea, the first Morning of Creation wrote
> What the last day of reckoning shall read.

Until very recently these words perhaps held for most of us, some seeing the fixing as fore-knowledge and predestination and others as the working of nature's eternal and inclusive laws. To be sure, novelty was a fact, but somehow it was negligible. To the orthodox theologian, everything was predestined. To the classical philosopher who looked at things *sub specie aeternitatis,* change was unreal. To the physical scientist, all apparent change was but the motion and recombination of eternal elements, all of which we might in time hope to foretell with certainty.

From this point of view, education was specific, consisting of training in distinct skills, habits, facts, etc. Thinking was soft-pedaled; in any event, it was limited to the few. Personality was slighted. Education was to make people efficient according to a prear-

---

[1] Franz Boas, *Anthropology and Modern Life*. W. W. Norton, New York, 1932, p. 132.

ranged plan. This fixedness in advance might reach also further. The system of social institutions was often conceived as already substantially fixed. Education, as stated by one writer, was to be thought of as a process "of transforming individuals so that they will conform to institutions." Schools were devised to "insure the transformation of every child so far as possible, into a being able and willing to conform to the social pattern of action and thought," this social pattern not being thought of as in process of change. Such a based-on-physics view of life was further elaborated and more clearly stated by another writer when he said that this "makes of education a kind of engineering. The engineer first plans the object he wishes to make—the house, the bridge, the electric transformer, the railroad bed. He sets up his plan in the form of a detailed blue print. . . . After he has perfected his blue print in every detail, his next step is to have the plan embodied in concrete materials. Now precisely the same procedure characterizes the new [scientific] education." We are not surprised to be further told by this writer that indoctrination is "one of the inevitable implications" of this kind of education because: "the problems the individuals will face in life are what they are, and one must come prepared to face them as they exist"; that "all education consists in a set of preadjustments for meeting the problem of life" and to plan accordingly we need "to know what the preadjustments are that the individuals in question will need"; that this "necessitates 'blue printing' the outcomes we want"; and that this blue print must indicate "the specific ideals, skills, bodies of information, attitudes of mind, prepared judgments, abilities to reason" that may be needed.

We do not have to suppose that any proponent of this position accepted all the implications inherent in it. (Fortunately, perhaps, people are not so consistent.) The tendencies are there, however, and school work has suffered accordingly.

But is life so fixed-in-advance that a "complete science of psychology," as one author suggests, is conceivable? Are our existing institutions so fixed and perfect that education exists simply or even primarily to transform individuals into conformity with them? Is life so fixed in advance that its problems and their solutions can be blue printed? Is the human personality to be constructed in the same mechanical fashion as the engineer makes a bridge? A generation ago when the science of physics seemed perfected and all phenomena were expected by scientists to come under the fatalism of its iron laws (psychology to be reduced to physiology, and physiology in its turn to chemistry and physics) it required hardihood for Peirce and James and Dewey to uphold the doctrine of an unsettled and contingent future. But they took the stand. And now physics itself renouncing practically all its former fundamental assumptions, has joined them. Out of better thinking there has come a practical consensus that actually novel events are still in the making.

We feel safe, then, in asserting that the future with which man deals is not fixed, but is in continual process. The world of affairs, both as a whole and in its significant details, gives us always a process of unique becoming. Life develops novelly, always mingling the familiar and unfamiliar. By means of the old and familiar, we see somewhat into the situation at hand and can, in some measure, control it. But there are limits beyond which we cannot see or control, and these limits are never known beforehand. These several characteristics of the total life process affect crucially the situation which education faces and so affect crucially our conception of education and how it should be managed. For one fundamental thing, widespread creative thinking follows as a necessary corollary. No mere fixed-in-advance responses could take care of our kind of world. Being novelly developing, it requires thinking and not mere habit to deal with it.

The opposed position (more or less set out above) is that the stream of life and affairs consists entirely of the recombination of eternal elements, seeming novelty being due solely to human ignorance. On this basis, expanding science would gradually encroach upon man's ignorance and master more and more of the combinations so as to foretell ever better what to expect and how to meet it. Education then would call, on the one hand, for experts to identify and foretell the problems and find the answers and, on the other, for teachers to pass on the expert-made answers to the rest of us.

The expert few would have need of thinking, the rest of us could rely sufficiently on the answer-habits drilled into us by our teachers.

During the generation just past those who adopted this position sought in varying degrees to impose that kind of education on our schools. But with novelty playing the continual part it does in ordinary life, it becomes impossible to foreknow the answers so that mere habit-drill will suffice. Take so simple a thing as crossing a busy street which has no traffic lights. No mother, however wise, could stay at home and make a non-thinking plan whereby her young child might safely cross this street when he comes to it. The problem cannot be solved in advance, but only on the spot in terms of what is then and there going on. The same is characteristic of life in all its significant aspects. Whether to start walking, where to walk and how fast, when to stop, are all matters of conscious control adjusted to the ends which one is pursuing.

The conclusion from this is an emphasis upon thinking as the rule of life. And education becomes primarily the process of building up good thinking with, of course, the correlative habits of acting obediently to the best thinking one can do. Acting upon thinking may then be taken as the unit element of the educative process. Our aim would accordingly be that the child have such varied opportunities of acting on thinking as would promise best to build up in him good thinking always with correlative appropriate action.

We have perhaps now seen enough to permit us to return to the preliminary statement of the activity position made earlier in this article. We see a world wherein history as a whole, and each individual process in particular, shows the fact of unique becoming. Since events develop novelly, we must think to manage them; and each one of us, whether of low or high intelligence, has continual need of thinking as we deal with the novel situations which life is continually meting out to us. Each such novel situation will have in it much that is old and familiar, and upon these habit, directed by thinking, can seize. We analyze, we plan accordingly, we try our plans, we watch them as they work out, we change them if need be. In this process we are using, as best we can, creative thinking at each stage—in the analysis, in the planning, in the executing, in the judging as we watch the plan work out, in the new changes introduced, in the backward judging as we seek to garner all the lessons which the experience has for us.

It is exactly this kind of experience, in which the learner faces thoughtfully and responsibly an actual situation, that the activity program seizes upon as the desirable and typical educational experience. What study means on the activity basis we have seen in the creative thinking which permeates this process from start to finish. How learning enters is easy to see.

Now one very significant conclusion appears. Whatever of an experience we accept to act on now or later, that we learn and it becomes part of us. And we learn it *as* and *only so far as* we accept it. If we accept it as a fact, albeit a disagreeable one, we learn it as a fact and we learn at the same time the attitude which counts it disagreeable. The standards of action which we accept to act on we learn, and they become part of us. If those I accept be high, I become a person of high standards. If low, I become a person of low standards. Whatever I accept to act on, that I learn and it becomes part of me. Moreover, I learn these things as holding under the conditions and reservations with which I accepted them. If, as a child, I accept a certain thing to act on it when mother is at hand but not to act on if no grown person is about to enforce it—if I do so accept it with these limitations, then I do so learn it.

This restatement of the law of effect reaches down to the heart of the activity program. What the proponents of this movement wish is such activity as *does* call out wholeheartedly the best that is in the child. If he thus accepts responsibility, then he learns responsibility and of the kind he accepted. If he discharges his responsibility badly, then we see plainer the kind and extent of his actual acceptance. For it is what he does really accept to act on that he learns and incorporates into his life and character. We accordingly wish, on the one hand, an educative situation which brings into play as fully as may be the child's varied resources. We wish, on the other hand, that he shall so accept willing responsibility for the enterprise that he shall, to the best of his ability, weigh and discriminate wisely before he accepts or rejects as he lives through the experience, because what *he* accepts, that *he* learns. And we wish his thoughtful weighing to permeate the activity from start to finish. We are particularly concerned with the standards he accepts to act on, for out of these his moral character as well as his everyday proficiency is largely built. It is then evident that we must stress pupil purposing because attitude more than anything else determines what the learner will accept, what standards he will act on as he weighs and accepts or rejects.

To say of such considerations as the foregoing that they "intensify individualism" or "enthrone a glorified hedonism" becomes an assertion beyond understanding. That child life holds the possibility of individualism and of hedonism is true (as later adult life too often and too painfully shows) but child life holds just as truly the opposites, as any teacher or parent well knows. What shall be called into play and accepted depends largely on the opportunity granted and the encouragement accorded. A program which consciously bases itself on thus calling out the best, as does the activity movement, would seem on the face of it to have a somewhat better chance at success than an alternative which concerns itself rather with the learning of subject matter than with the growth of the child.

It may be well now to say some things about particular criticisms leveled against the activity movement and about particular difficulties which actually present themselves.

The question of guidance and freedom seems perennial. The answer in general is easy, whatever difficulty specific situations may show. Since the child can only learn the response he makes and of these does learn only those which he accepts, we desire that the child shall have favorable opportunity for promising response to be called into action and, when any are so called out, that as far as possible he may then have the attitude to weigh them wisely and well. Both mean a general program of intelligently self-directed purposeful activity on the part of the children. The aim of the teacher is then so to act that the children may as they meet such situations grow most and best, all things considered. The teacher thus takes part with the children in helping them first to choose wisely what to undertake, then to manage that undertaking wisely, and finally to judge it wisely. If the teacher overdoes his part in helping to carry forward the enterprise, then the pupils are not only deprived of the opportunity of intelligent and responsible self-direction, but are liable to acquire a harmful dependency on the teacher or, contrariwise, develop a rebellious opposition. If, however, the teacher guides too little or unwisely, then the pupils may fail to think as well as they could and so again will fail to learn properly. Indeed, it easily happens that pupils left too much to themselves will engage in such hurtful experiences that these activities and the learning from them become specifically harmful.

What, then, is the conclusion for guidance? The opposed dangers just discussed give some idea of the considerations which the thoughtful teacher must take into account in deciding the manner and degree in which he should take his part in the class or pupil activity. As a rule, the teacher's part is that indirect but skilfull interposition which leads to better pupil thinking and stops short of teacher decision. This, in truth, is but the careful definition of *guidance*. The fact that there is a school at all sets a certain general limiting framework within which pupils may act. Beyond this, at particular times, the teacher may have to make and enforce specific regulations. At all times, whatever the teacher does—whether to guide, encourage, direct, or forbid—it is all done that the pupils may grow most and best along the most promising lines, all things considered. Among the proponents of the activity movement in this country, these lines lie in the direction of socially responsible self-direction. Since learning springs necessarily from pupil activity, the presumption lies on the side of child freedom; interference must justify itself. The teacher will take part by way of encouragment or refusal only in order to make child action more intelligent, more adequately self-directing, the test always being what the child is in fact learning. The teacher will work to bring ever more intelligent self-direction along lines of ever more adequate social responsibility.

The problems of pupil *versus* teacher initiative in the matter of instituting the educative experiences (activities) is another question that is often discussed. Logically, this is included in the foregoing; but a few words to the immediate point may help. From learning considerations it were better, other things being equal, for the pupils to initiate their own projects. In such, they should find excellent opportunity for creative thinking and for the practical weighing of consequences and, at the same time, they should be acquiring intelligent responsibility. These lines of development are what we wish. But, without teacher guidance, pupils will often fail to grow satisfactorily along these lines. Almost surely the teacher should take part in the discussion (with the precautions already discussed) of which project next to undertake, else the pupils will not see as well as they might the possibilities and dangers of the situation. It may, at times, be wise for the teacher to make a very specific proposal and even, in the extreme case, to compel its acceptance. But if the teacher thus interposes, he must know the dangers in what he does and see clearly the advantage to be gained. The chief dangers from too much teacher participation seem to be that the pupils will not enter so wholeheartedly into what they do (and so lose somewhat of the best learning conditions) and that they may build again the devastating habits of waiting to be told and of doing as little as possible. Intelligent initiative is a great social and individual asset, and is not given adequately by nature alone. As matters stand, we cannot expect it in most of our pupils unless we consistently cultivate it. And this means, in general, that we must give it fair chance to act itself out. This, then, should be our aim and rule.

It is an easy next step to the much disputed question of creative ability. How many have this ability? Is it widespread or is it rare? And in what does it show itself? Only in music, literature, and the fine arts? Or in all lines of human endeavor? All these questions have already been implicitly answered in the discussion on creative thinking, but it will perhaps again be well to make some specific statements. First, we cannot here limit the term "creation" to a contribution to the world's stock; that is, to those few outputs which constitute in worth positive additions to the world stock over and above anything previously existing. Psychologically speaking, any one creates who devises a response that is new to *him*. But no such creation is entirely new. Always, even with the utmost genius, there enters the factor of suggestion from some prior form or source. Thus, along any chosen line, we may form an imitation-creation scale: at the upper end, the highest known proportion of creation to prior existing model or suggestion; at the lower end, the least of this creation and the greatest known amount of mere adoption and imitation. On such a scale we can readily arrange that all men should somewhere fall, thus forming probably an approximation to the normal distribution curve. We all create in greater or less degree. Specifically, there appears no just reason for limiting creation to music, literature, and the fine arts. Statesmanship can show its scale and so can cooking, plowing, generalship, and science. There is no line of human activity that does not so distribute itself.

If we are really interested in helping pupils to grow, it will help wonderfully not to divide men into just two groups—the sheep and the goats—those who can create and those who cannot. It is a blasphemy to deny in advance some possibility of creating even to the lowliest. All who do the normal things of life are called upon every day to create their own lives and to help with those about them. Moreover, effectual creating can be cultivated; and life, both social and individual, has need of all the creation that can be mustered.

As we speak thus favorably of freedom and initiative and pupil purposing, many get frightened and wonder about the necessary order and effectual method of learning. "Are we going to risk," these ask, "the intellectual gains our pupils now enjoy in behalf of a scheme which offers no certain order or fact of learning? If order be disregarded, if pupils do not learn things in the right order, will not their minds grow chaotic? Can we take such risks?" To these questions, there are two answers. First, as matters now stand, the actual learning achieved in the ordinary school is none too good or great. With such an outcome in relation to the possibilities we can perhaps afford to take a risk. Second, but more fundamentally—save in a few things that easily take care of themselves, like counting before number combinations or addition before multiplication—there is no known basis for claiming that the order in which things are learned has any effect on the order in which they are organized for use. Thinking is so related to living that each one gradually builds his conceptions and his organizations out of the experiences of life so as to meet the needs of life. My conception of a dog, if I may speak personally, began with my earliest experiences of dogs and has been added to and corrected as I have met and faced other and different dogs and dog behavior. With me, this conception remains now fairly static and largely on this common-sense basis. The reason why I have no more scientific conception of dogs is that I have little need and consequently few opportunities to change my work-a-day notions into more scientific conceptions. And I have no special regrets about the lack. My life's needs on this point seem well met. Along other lines, however—say, in psychology—my experience has been different. I have been stimulated to think much more deeply and broadly than about dogs, and my conceptions in this field have been carried (I hope) to a correspondingly higher stage of development. But the order of learning has had nothing whatever to do with the order in which I hold it for use. The difference has been, more immediately, in the amount and quality of thinking I have done and, less immediately, in the demand and opportunity for better thinking. The process of organization, however, is psychologically the same in both cases—simply a matter of the organization and generalization for use of my successive experiences. If the actual organizations are different, it is because the demands have been different and my thinking has built itself accordingly.

What will count then with our young people is not the order and arrangement of subject matter, but the kind of lives they lead and the kind of thinking they are accordingly called upon to do. So far as schools go, the teacher is a great factor in the matter. In the activity school the teacher must encourage varied living and good thinking in connection, taking care that connections with preceding matters be made and that new leads be noted. The results should be cumulative and, in time (if things go well), the varied thought connections and leads will build new interests somewhat higher in intellectual character which will demand and receive attention on their own account. The teacher, knowing more of the general ground and of its possibilities, will guide to these ends. Organization of thought on the activity basis should, then, be simultaneously matters of wise teacher guidance and of pupil interest and responsibility. With each consciously cared for, the possibilities are much better than where reliance is placed on organization worked out in text-books or in curricula, no matter how expertly these be made. After all, while one can get help and suggestion from others, the conceptions and the organization one uses are those which he himself has made. It must be so. It cannot be otherwise.

From this the question easily arises as to what use the activity program will make of books and specific subject matter. The answer is unequivocal. We are concerned first with each child that he grow as a person and into proper human relationships. We wish to use books and subject matter but only as means to continuous child growth and living as an end. And we are not apprehensive as to results. Under the activity program, intelligently directed, more books will be used and more subject matter will be acquired than under the older program. We wish our children to become intelligent about the world around us, while they learn to enrich life and also (so some of us at any rate are thinking) learn to criticize our institutional life so as the more intelligently to control it. All of this we desire, as previously stated, for the sake of and on the bases of simultaneous growth in intelligent self-direction and appropriate social outlook. Therefore, as children undertake any enterprise and try to deal with it intelligently, they will need help from various sources. Books will furnish one valuable aid. Most of our pupils will come from homes where reading is at least expected of them. The teachers, also, will expect reading and encourage it. The danger is that parents and teachers alike may too quickly advise books, forgetting that these are valuable not as the signs of an education but as the means to life. In this as in many other matters, appetite should not be forced. If books are used because they are needed they will more likely be appreciated accordingly. In this the teacher and the brighter pupils can set a tone which will help others to give the books a fairer chance. Once the mind is willing and the teacher wise, most pupils will come readily to the use of books. The appetite for reading easily grows. We must not expect that all will become great readers, but we can easily improve over what now obtains.

The discussion for books holds also for subject matter. By "subject matter" we mean here simply knowledge conceived as instrumental to thought and endeavor. If the school be successful and pupils live in fact rich and varied lives, there will necessarily arise many and varied demands for knowledge. Here, as usual, the teacher and the better pupils will lead the way and set the growing standards, but the others may truly share the life and its inherent demands. If knowledge and standards thus be not forced from the outside, but are shown not only to fit into life but actually to inhere in it to enrich it, then the attitudes of pupils are favorable and the seeking of knowledge and the building of appropriate standards are both natural and easy. True it is that home and community standards will continue to exercise their influence (thus setting a serious problem for a new and wider adult education) but the procedures here advocated indicate promising lines of school endeavor. Collings' experience in the Missouri rural schools, to quote a carefully recorded instance, bears out the promise.[2]

Closely connected with subject matter in the minds of many teachers is the question of drill. Because meaningless drill has proved so repellent, many teachers fear any sharing of decisions regarding this with pupils. The crux lies in the word "meaningless." Let the actual situation of any child call to him for drill and there seems no lack of willingness to engage in it, as we see in the case of small boys with their first roller skates or of larger boys with their catching and batting. Even clearer, perhaps, is the case of very young children with their repetition of words and phrases and noise-making operations, often to the great annoyance of unsympathetic adults. One could without difficulty make out a good case that the child is a "natural" repeater. But learning is far from being mere repetition.

---

[2] Ellsworth Collings, *An Experiment with a Project Curriculum*. The Macmillan Co., New York, 1927.

Let but the experiences of the child arouse sufficient interest in and regard for consequences, and repetition as such retires into the background. Felt connection is the best basis of acquisition. We used to think that much mechanically repetitive drill was necessary to learning such things as spelling, writing, and number combinations. Now it appears that bare repetition, without any supporting connection or check, carries no learning effect; while, for the normal child, a sufficiently varied and interesting school life will by its inherent use of spelling, for example, teach ninety per cent of what may be needed. And similar conditions appear to hold in the case of most, if not all, the so-called mechanical operations. The remaining ten or more per cent seems best cared for on the basis of individual treatment, the teacher studying each case on its merits and helping the individual child to map out his own remedial treatment. Here, as elsewhere, the building of a common standard of accepted ideals is a great help. The main point of the whole matter is that everything done be meaningful to the doer. Let drill come only after the need has been set up and the meaning connection made clear. In the degree that these be attained, the rest becomes easy.

Implicit in everything so far said has been a regard for "the whole child." Because some affect to find difficulty with this conception, a word or two of explanation seems called for. The conception of "the whole child" carries two implications which at bottom agree: one, that we wish at no time to disregard the varied aspects of child life; the other, that the child as organism properly responds as one unified whole. From the first, we must not teach the child to read at the expense of his eyes, or cultivate his intellect at the expense of his soul. Rather must we know, as the second implication explicitly demands, that the child is in any typical case acting simultaneously under the varied heads of his possibilities. He thinks, he feels, he acts (moves physically), and at the same time his body is physiologically engaged in its varied ways. We must know this and take due account of the consequences that flow from the fact. Whatever the child does carries some learning effect to all the connected aspects of his being that are engaged. So far as taking thought can better care for all these effects and their combined total, so far are we as teachers under obligation to take that thought and act accordingly.

To say that the biological organism acts as one unity is by no means to deny that persons do build varying and possibly opposed selves and that they act at one time from one self, and at a different time from another self. Still less is it to assert that all one's resources, all one's different habits, skills, knowledges, attitudes, etc., act simultaneously as the organism faces a situation. This would be so complete a denial of the proposition under consideration (i.e., that the organism acts as a unity) that one wonders how an intelligent critic could ever suggest such an objection. The organism as it faces a situation, say a cat trying to catch a bird, brings all its available resources to bear and these act together to reinforce and support each other. The same cat facing a threatening dog would again bring all its available resources to bear in an analogously coöperating fashion. Since the task in the two cases is different, the resources called into play are somewhat different. In each case the cat's organism acts as one whole and unity, all responding parts and aspects coöperating not only simultaneously but also from stage to stage. To say in the face of these considerations, as one writer has done, that the phrase "the whole child" is "an empty verbalism" seems a strangely unscientific statement to make, indicative perhaps of the reluctance of his science to admit of personality in preference to atomistic elements. To the proponents of the activity movement the phrase carries a principle pregnant with positive resulting guidance.

The principle of "the whole child" and of the organism acting as a whole leads easily to the problem of the integration of personality. When a person faces a situation of one clearly defined type and learns to deal satisfactorily with it, he does, in some measure, reconstruct his personality on the basis of what is therein learned. If the situation recurs with ordinary variations, the personality may in time be appreciably rebuilt so that a characteristic attitude or set, corresponding to that type of situation, is readily assumed when such a situation presents itself. It may, however, happen that one situation contains within itself contradictory demands which the person cannot harmonize. Under such conditions, he may accept one line of demand and reject the other. If he does so, and it works out acceptably, he will grow to be that kind of person. He might, however, so far as we see, have accepted the other line of demand and so built himself into *that* kind of person. In each case the organism has acted as a whole and built a pattern accordingly. But a third outcome is possible. The person, while recognizing the conflict between the two sets of demand, may still—especially under compulsion—try to meet both. A child will thus do one thing while the teacher is looking and another when the teacher does not see. In such case, the child's conduct is outwardly of one kind but inwardly of another. In this and other cases of reacting to conflicting stimuli, there results an internal conflict. Both lines of conduct call on the organism to act as a whole but in different ways. The two ways being incompatible, the person's efforts in either direction are interfered with by the demands from the other direction. His personality is thus distraught. He is on the road toward disintegration.

Many among us—many more than we are commonly aware of —suffer mild cases of this sort of thing. So widely true is this, particularly in a civilization so chaotic as ours, that what we think of as a "normal person" (that is, the rule and average) is probably far below the true normal life of zest and happiness which most of us might enjoy. Besides this, however, there are many cases of severe maladjustment. The "problem child" has become a stark reality to all schools and to many families. This is no place to discuss mental hygiene, but it seems safe to say that all ordinary cases at least illustrate the failure to face life's situations with reasonable success. A well managed régime of purposeful activity freed from artificial and external demands of subject-matter requirements promises not only the best preventive of personality maladjustment but often also furnishes an indispensable part of any adequate remediable treatment. To learn to pursue worthy ends with honest study and appropriate action is nature's road to mental health.

Finally, does the activity program imply any one social philosophy of life in preference to others? Various critics have not hesitated to answer the question, some contending that the activity program is but the handmaiden of a selfish individualism; others, that it makes for anarchy. The whole foregoing discussion has consciously rejected both of these in favor of a more socialized outlook. The question thus becomes more explicit: Is there any one philosophy of life inherent in the activity outlook? If so, what is it? If not, is the connection of this outlook with one philosophy rather than another quite arbitrary?

The answer seems to be that there are selective implications, the activity program being more congenial with certain philosophies than with others. But the activity principle does not of itself alone suffice to determine one's philosophy of life. A philosophy is necessarily too inclusive to be determined by any one principle; it must take into account all known aspects of life. For instance, if again I may speak regarding myself, since early adulthood I have accepted the democratic view of life, and with this the activity outlook has seemed quite congenial. Recognizing grave evils in our industrial life, I favored for many years a great extension of "industrial democracy" into our economic régime but conceived this as continuing substantially within the framework of a laissez faire competition for profits, only greatly reformed. Of late years, I have come to believe that no mere reformation of this framework will suffice. A fundamental remaking of our economic system seems necessary so that men shall no longer be compelled to work against each other but may rather be permitted and encouraged—and if a recalcitrant minority requires it, be compelled—to coöperate for the common good. Whether this shift of view be a change of philosophy depends, of course, on definition. It certainly does involve a very great change in certain attitudes. But for me, at any rate, democracy and the activity outlook still abide and concur, neither curtailed to fit into a straiter scheme but both freed to coöperate on a wider scale for a fuller life for all.

Possibly, then, the answer as regards the activity outlook is closely bound up with democracy. Any one who genuinely accepts

Spencer divides life into the several leading kinds of activity. The five kinds of activity in order of importance are those (1) that directly minister to self-preservation; (2) which, by securing the necessities of life, indirectly minister to self-preservation; (3) that have for their end the rearing and discipline of offspring; (4) that are involved in the maintenance of proper social and political relations; and (5) that make up the leisure part of life, devoted to the gratification of the tastes and feelings. Spencer then proposes that the curriculum be designed to prepare people for performing these most important activities.

Other people, too, have categorized life's activities, though somewhat differently from Spencer, and have proposed that the curriculum be focused on them.* A comparison of these various sets of categories shows how they are all quite similar in substance and intent.

Stratemeyer's curriculum focus through its categories and intentions thus bears a strong resemblance to previous and subsequent proposals based on life's everyday concerns. But Stratemeyer goes beyond categorization by specifically establishing a psychological and pedagogical rationale for utilizing persistent life situations. Her aim is to use these situations to achieve curriculum flexibility, balance, motivation, continuity, and transfer of learning.

Careful reading will show just how Stratemeyer expects to achieve her goal. Also, the relation between Stratemeyer's focus and those of Dewey (Chapter 1), Metcalf and Hunt (Chapter 8), and Hand (Chapter 4) deserves the reader's investigation. In like manner the difference between Stratemeyer and King and Brownell (Chapter 5) warrants explicit noting.

---

* The famous Commission on the Reorganization of Secondary Education suggested in 1918 that the function of education was to help people live well in the following seven key areas: health, command of fundamental processes, worthy home membership, vocation, citizenship, worthy use of leisure time, and ethical character. These are the commonly called Seven Cardinal Principles. Yet there is no evidence that the Commission directly suggested that the curriculum be organized around these key areas of life rather than around the traditional subjects. The Joint Committee on Curriculum established by the Department of Supervision and Directors of Instruction and the Society for Curriculum Study in 1937 did actually propose a curriculum organized around eight "areas of living": living in the home, leisure, citizenship, organized group life, consumption, production, communication, and transportation.

In the curriculum focused on learner's interests and the persistent life situations which are a part of those concerns, the nature of society, the nature of the learner, and the way in which learning takes place are viewed as central in curriculum development. Society provides the framework within which children and youth live and learn, and inevitably affects what they bring to school and the ways in which they put their school experiences to work. The kind of society from which learners come gives direction to the values they seek to achieve as they share with others the task of building their country and their world. If that task is to be prosecuted constructively a curriculum proposal must take into account the capacities of the individual, how he matures, and the way he learns. Not to do so risks wasting valuable hours of child and teacher time on concepts or skills that could be acquired much more effectively at another stage of development. More serious is the possibility of "teaching" skills, concepts, and facts that do not make their anticipated contribution to effective living.

THE EVERYDAY CONCERNS OF THE LEARNER ARE THE STARTING POINT

Children and youth develop at different rates, have widely differing backgrounds, and come to school with varying interests. Their concerns are many—how to make a model airplane fly, what to feed a pet turtle, whom to elect as captain of the baseball team, why paints dry out, how to interpret the headlines in the daily paper, how to get a bicycle license, what it means to fly faster than sound,

Adapted by the author with the permission of the publisher from Stratemeyer, Forkner, McKim, Passow, Chap. 5, "A Proposal for Designing a Curriculum for Living in Our Time," in *Developing a Curriculum for Modern Living* (New York: Teachers College Press), copyright 1957.

Persistent Life Situations Recur
Throughout the Life of the Individual

The same persistent situation reappears again and again in the everyday concerns of the individual at different stages of his development. *Therefore, the child or youth who is helped to see that similar situations recur in his everyday living can apply what he has learned in one situation to another and can test in experience the worth of his former learning.*

Managing money is a life situation that recurs again and again.

A **five- or six-year-old** manages money as he goes on an errand to a neighborhood store, and as he decides how much of his allowance to spend on candy, put aside for Sunday School, or save in his bank.

At **eight or ten** the child also meets the same persistent life situation when he buys at the store, shares in decisions about spending family funds, puts money in the local or school bank, repays money borrowed from parents.

At **fifteen** the young person also buys at the store. He decides where to buy so that he can get the best merchandise for his money, what the price differences are on similar materials, what labels on materials mean. His everyday concerns may include budgeting his allowance, deciding whether to ask for a larger allowance, seeking jobs to supplement his allowance so that he can satisfy his needs.

The **adult** also deals with problems of money management in making purchases and he meets many of the same everyday concerns faced by the adolescent. He deals with larger amounts of money and more complicated situations—deciding when to purchase commodities wholesale, getting information from various agencies for consumer protection, financing a home or a business, providing funds for the education of offspring, providing security for later life.

Persistent Life Situations Take On New
Meaning as the Individual Matures

Different aspects of persistent life situations become meaningful to the individual as he matures. *Therefore, the child or youth who is helped to deal with persistent life situations as they reappear in more complex form grows in insight into the problems he faces and widens and extends his understandings and concepts.*

Being accepted in a group is a persistent life situation that all individuals face, but acceptance has different meanings at different ages.

For the **six-year-old** being accepted in a group may mean getting others to play with him, knowing when and how to share his toys and other possessions, being allowed to use the toys of other children, being chosen by his group to do certain jobs. The six-year-old wants everyone to like him, but on his own terms.

The **ten-year-old** has some understanding of the feelings and wishes of others. He is willing for others to be considered, provided his wishes are not neglected. He is willing to have his friend made captain of the team if he himself is chosen to be on the team. Special problems of acceptance arise in working on teams or committees with members of the opposite sex.

For a **fifteen-year-old** both social customs and taboos must be carefully observed to gain acceptance in a peer group. Acceptance for the adolescent also means maintaining the security of close family ties while achieving acceptance by the new groups that are becoming a part of his developing independence. Among the everyday situations that he faces as he seeks to establish himself in his group are deciding when to break with community customs, resolving conflicts between the values of family and of friends, deciding whether to seek a class office, and deciding how long to observe a code not accepted by others in the group.

An **adult** continues to face the persistent life situation of being an accepted member of groups. He must learn how to make a constructive contribution to a community group; how to develop satisfactory group membership in church, club, or business when there are differences in race, religious affiliation, socio-economic status; how to relate himself to his family group; how to help his children make a positive contribution to the family group.

Many Persistent Life Situations May Be Involved In A Given Immediate Situation

Almost any everyday concern includes more than one persistent life situation. The number of persistent life situations included will

duction, and distribution of tools and equipment will have meaning must grow out of the learner's own experience.

Working with different racial and religious groups is another persistent life situation that learners meet in a variety of ways. The meaning of this situation may differ in homogeneous and heterogeneous groups.

In a **heterogeneous population** the problem of religious differences may arise when certain children are absent from school because of special religious holidays or when they observe or comment on food practices. Or the immediate circumstances might be a reference to special religious schools. Whatever the everyday concern, its meaning to the learner who is a member of the minority group involved is quite different from its meaning to members of the majority group.

In a **homogeneous population,** where children have similar racial, national, religious, and economic backgrounds, understandings of differences among groups will come about differently. Within such groups many situations will arise which call for consideration and understanding of other racial, religious, social, and economic groups. There will be situations such as those created by radio, television, and news comments on federal aid to religious schools, reports on cases of racial discrimination, a local election issue relating to legislation in the interest of minority groups.

Persistent Life Situations Are a Part of All Aspects of the Learner's Daily Life

Persistent life situations are faced by the learner at home, at school, in the neighborhood, at church, at the movies, at camp, and in the host of other places where he works and plays. The same persistent life situation may be a part of several experiences which a learner has in any one day. *Therefore, children and youth who are helped to relate and integrate experiences—to see the same persistent life situation in everyday activities in the school, home, and community . . .*

will develop consistent ways of behaving as learnings gained in one situation are used in another will find in-school learning functionally useful out of school and vice versa

Maximum growth is possible only when the dominant agencies guiding the learner's activities—home, school, church, community— coordinate their efforts. The school must view the learner's total experience and the curriculum must be responsive to the contributions of other agencies and learning experiences.

Using safety measures is a persistent life situation that occurs:

> In the **home** when deciding where to keep playthings and tools, when using tools and machines, when using matches or caring for fires, when repairing household appliances, when deciding where to play, when deciding where to keep medicines.

> In the **school** when using tools and equipment, when deciding where to keep tools and how to use them, when participating in fire drills, when working with traffic patrol, when participating in active sports.

> In the **community** when riding a bicycle or driving a car, when crossing streets, when swimming, when picnicking in woods, when taking action on legislation regarding safety measures.

Dealing with success and failure is a persistent life situation that occurs:

> In the **home** when a favorite toy breaks or a pet dies, when parental restrictions upset plans, when brothers or sisters tease, when parents praise a job well done, when report cards come home, when constructing a playhouse or taking a paper route.

> In the **neighborhood** when participating in such social gatherings as dances at the community center and birthday parties; when taking part in recreational activities such as playing ball, tennis, and card games; when participating in club activities through voluntary effort— serving as chairman, officer, or committee member.

> In the **school** when representing a class in making an announcement in assembly; when making a report, responding to a question, taking an examination; when participating in a class play, playing on

and widening of concepts/generalizations as new aspects of persistent life situations are dealt with. A curriculum which helps learners to deal with varied aspects of the same persistent life situation recognizes that . . .

> children and youth seek to learn those things that their maturity and experience make meaningful to them

> an optimal moment of learning for one person may not be the same as that for another

> in meeting new situations the individual draws upon the generalizations which have emerged from previous experience

sequence is determined by the changing aspects of persistent life situations as the learner moves from childhood into the full responsibilities of adulthood.

school and community experiences *are related* because the same persistent life situations are faced in the home, at school, in the neighborhood, at church, and in the varied other places where the learner works and plays. A curriculum built with regard for the fact that the same persistent life situation is met in both in-school and out-of-school activities of children and youth recognizes that the school as the delegated educational agency must . . .

> consider the total educational program needed by learners in the given community

> be keenly aware of those things which other agencies are helping him to learn

> vary its own leadership to recognize the best use of community resources

useful *facts, generalizations, skills,* and *attitudes are learned.* The curriculum which helps individuals deal with the same persistent life situation as it is faced in different forms and under different circumstances affords maximum opportunity to generalize and build skills and attitudes to use in recurring situations. Understandings, skills, and attitudes expand as persistent life situations are met in new experiences.

A SUMMARY LOOK

A curriculum which helps learners to deal with varied aspects of the same persistent life situation and with the range of these recurring situations builds on knowledge of the learner and the learning process.

Children and youth learn those things that are related to their purposes. The proposed curriculum, therefore, . . .

> starts with the everyday concerns and experiences of learners
>
> deals with those aspects of persistent life situations appropriate to the learners' background and maturity
>
> helps learners deal with the one or more persistent situations which are a part of the immediate situation and most closely related to their needs
>
> provides opportunities for learners to share in the selection and development of experiences

Individuals differ in interests, needs, abilities, and growth patterns. The proposed curriculum, therefore, . . .

> provides varied experiences for individuals and for groups from one year to another
>
> helps individuals work on different aspects of the same persistent life situation which is a part of a group concern
>
> helps individuals work on different persistent life situations which are a part of the group's immediate problem
>
> gives recognition to the right of individuals to bring different purposes to a common experience and to use different ways of working

the curriculum can be responsive to the interests and abilities of individual learners through all-class, small-group, and individual activities

the curriculum can be developed in terms of the particular situations of most concern to individuals and still enable them to grow in skills, understandings, and competencies needed by all persons

both a flexible curriculum and one which provides for growth in ability to deal with common and universal problems can be provided

Because many persistent life situations may be involved in an immediate situation . . .

such situations can be used to develop a variety of skills and competencies

individual needs and interests can be provided for through work on group problems

emphases can be adjusted so that the needs and abilities of the individual learner will determine which of the several persistent life situations will receive the greatest attention

children and youth can be helped to understand interrelationships among persistent life situations

Because dealing with persistent life situations calls for action based on understanding . . .

maximum opportunity can be afforded to generalize and to use basic understandings and accepted values in new situations

learners can be helped to acquire knowledge, concepts, and skills under circumstances which provide optimum encouragement to use these learnings

learnings tend to remain at a high level of competence, since recurring situations call for their repeated use

learners can be helped to acquire problem-solving skills essential in a world of change

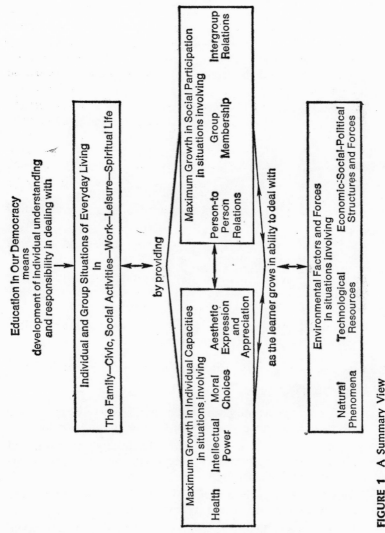

Education In Our Democracy
means
development of individual understanding
and responsibility in dealing with

Individual and Group Situations of Everyday Living
In
The Family—Civic, Social Activities—Work—Leisure—Spiritual Life

by providing

Maximum Growth in Individual Capacities
in situations involving

Health   Intellectual   Moral   Aesthetic
Power   Choices   Expression and Appreciation

Maximum Growth in Social Participation
in situations involving

Person-to Person Relations   Group Membership   Intergroup Relations

as the learner grows in ability to deal with

Environmental Factors and Forces
in situations involving

Natural Phenomena   Technological Resources   Economic-Social-Political Structures and Forces

FIGURE 1 A Summary View

lums is real and strong. (See the last part of the article by Bellack, Chapter 6, in reference to this point.)

Therefore, it is worthwhile for comparison's sake, complimentariness, and further elucidation of this type of alternative to present the four explicit principles set forth by Harold Alberty, a chief proponent of core. These principles constitute the basis of Alberty's curriculum proposal:

1. The ideals and values of democracy and the implied characteristics of personality essential to good citizenship, provide the direction for curriculum reorganization.

2. The needs, problems, and interests of the adolescent, which grow out of his interaction with the culture, provides the basis for the learning activities which make up the curriculum.

3. The common needs of the adolescent can best be met by the teacher-student planned learning units based upon broad problem areas which draw upon all pertinent fields of knowledge, and which provide for most of the values, understandings, abilities, and skills needed by all.

4. The specialized needs of the adolescent can best be met through interest areas closely related to the common needs aspect of the curriculum.*

The reader should also consider the connections between Hand and Wise (Chapter 7) and Metcalf and Hunt (Chapter 8) not only in their rejections of the traditional curriculum but also in their formulations. With regard to the utilization of the academic disciplines it is well to compare Hand with Bellack (Chapter 6) and King and Brownell (Chapter 5).

Once again, is Hand's case "unassailable"?

---

* Harold Alberty, "A Proposal for Reorganizing the High-School Curriculum on the Basis of a Core Program," *Progressive Education* 28, No. 2 (November, 1950): 57–61.

<><><><><><><><><><><><><><><><><><><><><><><><><><><><><><>

The case for the "common learnings" course is, in my opinion, unassailable. The argument can be simply, though not briefly, put. It runs somewhat as follows:

We start with a two part premise, the validity of which is beyond dispute: (1) That it is the responsibility of the secondary school to aid society in carrying on the basic social processes which can be neglected only at the certain cost of societal retrogression and decay, and (2) that it is also the responsibility of the secondary school to nurture youth in reference to all types of wholesome growth—to aid them in performing their developmental tasks and in meeting their other practical problems of "getting along" in an adequate manner. It might be added that this second responsibility can be neglected only at the certain cost of personal inadequacies (and consequent frustrations) in the pupils supposedly being "educated" by the school.

Let us make more specific each of these two responsibilities, in the order named.

If it is to escape commitment to the wastebasket of history, any given society in any given time or place must successfully carry forward certain basic social processes. It must enable its population to make a living. It must provide physical security for its members (in our time, this means guaranteeing the peace). It must keep its population healthy and vigorous, and safeguard its members against accidents and disease. It must develop, wisely utilize, and conserve its natural resources. It must rear and educate its young. It must enable its population to satisfy its spiritual and aesthetic impulses. It must provide recreation for its members. It must provide sufficient "social cement" (a body of commonly held beliefs and aspirations) to afford societal integration. And it must so organize and govern its popu-

"The Case for the Common Learnings Course" by Harold C. Hand is reprinted with permission from *Science Education* 32 (February, 1948): 5–11.

a job, learning how to buy wisely, learning how to prevent accidents and care for one's health, learning how to improve one's personal appearance, acquiring the good manners associated with poise and self-confidence, learning how to get along happily and effectively with other people, acquiring good work habits and learning how to "stick to" a job, learning how to communicate (speak, write, read, listen) more effectively and enjoyably, learning how to select and to enjoy good books, newspapers, magazines, motion pictures and radio programs, learning how to sing or play a musical instrument and to enjoy good music, learning some handicraft or other enjoyable manual skill, learning enjoyable games and sports, developing a hobby, developing intellectual interests and becoming a more cultivated person, becoming literate in reference to community, national, and world problems and developing the interest and ability to participate in resolving them, and preparing for a happy marriage, intelligent home management and wise parenthood.

Unless our educational program is to be of the ivory tower variety, all of the learning experiences connoted by these practical life-needs of youth must be provided by our secondary schools.

Perhaps we have said enough to demonstrate the validity of the two-part premise with which we began; namely, that it is the responsibility of the secondary school (1) to aid society in carrying forward the basic social processes essential for societal survival and (2) to give all the types of practical help which youth need in order to "get along" adequately. At any rate, we shall rest this part of our case at this point.

The next part of the case for the common learnings course will consist of a demonstration of the fact that *both* of these two responsibilities are seriously neglected, and inevitably so, by the traditional broad field area approach (the curriculum structured as English, social studies, science, mathematics, modern languages, etc.—the traditional subjects of "general education").

Let us first note some of the evidence bearing on the established fact of this neglect. The most biting general appraisal is that made by the Educational Policies Commission:

"Setting: A democracy struggling against strangulation in an era marked by confused loyalties in the political realm, by unrest and deprivation, by much unnecessary ill health, by high-pressure propaganda, by war, by many broken or ill-adjusted homes, by foolish spending, by high crime rates, by bad housing, and by a myriad of other urgent real human problems. And what are the children in this school, in this age, in this culture, learning? They are learning that the square of the sum of two numbers equals the sum of their squares plus twice their product: that Millard Fillmore was the thirteenth President of the United States and held office from January 10, 1850 to March 4, 1853; that the capital of Honduras is Tegucigalpa; that there were two Peloponnesian wars and three Punic wars; that Latin verbs meaning to command, obey, please, displease, serve, resist, and the like, take the dative; and that a gerund is a neuter verbal noun used in the oblique cases of the singular and governing the same case as its verb." [2]

That this impressionistic appraisal is probably uncomfortably close to the mark is attested by the findings of the New York Regents Inquiry, a study in which the investigators went directly to school—leaving youth to find out what they believed, knew, and did. It was found that the high school characteristically gave little or no help to these youth in finding jobs, that these pupils typically had educational and vocational plans which were strikingly unrealistic, that they showed little discrimination in selecting radio programs and motion pictures, that they voluntarily read little other than mediocre books—and very few even of these, that they were seriously deficient in their knowledge of the facts and problems with which citizens should be concerned, that they were uninformed about social conditions even in their own communities, that they had little tolerance for new ways of dealing with social problems, and that the longer they had been in school the less disposed they were to do anything for the common good.

---

[2] Educational Policies Commission. *The Purposes of Education in American Democracy*, p. 147.

logic of real-life-problem-solving vs. the inner logic of standard subjects which at best admits of but incidental attention to such problems—efforts to "functionalize" the traditional high school subjects invariably and inevitably result in asking the teacher simultaneously to serve two contrarily-oriented masters. That this is frustrating in the extreme, there can be little doubt—as any number of intelligent and conscientious teachers will testify. What is more important, the traditional master almost invariably wins out in this unhappy and unequal struggle—to the educational neglect of society and youth, as we have demonstrated. If the course is labeled "English," or "social studies" or any other name identified with a recognized body of more or less standard subject matter, the teacher is conscience-stricken unless he gets across at least a respectable minimum of whatever this subject matter may be. This he will usually do regardless of the fate of the problems with which he is also supposed to be dealing. But this neglect of problems also induces feelings of guilt, it must be recognized. What this adds up to is scarcely a recipe for good mental health.

Let us suppose, however, that by some magic this conflict of inner logics could be resolved and that every one of the traditional subjects or broad field areas could be 100% functionalized. Even with such a program of 100% functionalized subjects, it would still be impossible for any school to discharge either of the two responsibilities noted in our premise. This would be true because no societal or youth problem of any real significance can be understood, much less resolved, by appeal to the resources which any one of the subject matter fields could afford. Instead, every such problem requires various of the resources of several of the usual subject fields plus certain others not afforded by any broad field area now included in the high school curriculum. Let the skeptical reader take any important real-life problem he chooses and in terms of subject fields trace out what it would take to make youth even literate in reference to the problem. Then let him note what it would take to equip youth to effect the individual and/or social action necessary to resolve this problem.

From what has just been noted, it might mistakenly be assumed that the two basic responsibilities laid down in our premise could be discharged if two, three, or more of the traditional subjects were combined in some manner and teams of say English, social studies, and science teachers were to instruct jointly. This brings into conflict not two but eight inner logics; namely, that of English vs. that of social and personal problem solving, social studies vs. problem solving, science vs. problem solving, English vs. social studies, English vs. science, and social studies vs. science. So long as there is any presumption that respectable minima of English, social studies and science will be taught in such hybrid situations (in schools where this type of programming is practised the work is not uncommonly separately recorded in the front office as English, social studies and science), the stage would appear to be set for teacher vs. teacher as well as standard subject matter vs. problem solving conflicts of no inconsequential order. We are guilty of understatement when we say that this does *not* appear to be the way to meet the twin responsibilities laid down in our premise.

Nothing remains except to provide in each year of the high school a required offering which makes a *direct* attack on societal and youth problems, which has no responsibility other than this, which is called by a name in no way identified with any existing body of standard subject matter, and which utilizes whatever resources it takes to do the job. This is precisely what is connoted by the term "common learnings course" as employed in this paper.

Of what "whole" should this new offering be a part? In other words, what would the total operating program of the secondary school which included such a required offering look like? Here is the "total picture" as it is visualized:

1. Common Learnings Course

   Two hours per day in all secondary school years through grade eleven. One hour per day in grade twelve. Required of all pupils.

2. Health and Physical Education Activities

One hour per day in all years. Required of all pupils.

3. Standard Specialized Subjects (English, biology, mathematics, vocational courses, etc.)

   Elective under guidance except in exceptional cases. Required only on the basis of demonstrated pupil-need in individual cases.

4. Guidance and Personnel Services

   (What is ordinarily called group guidance would be included in number one above). Special provisions as needed for exceptional pupils. Testing program. Counseling of referrals. Record keeping and reporting.

5. Activities Period

   One hour daily, alternately given to clubs, assemblies, intramurals, band, orchestra, glee club, etc.

Before turning to a somewhat detailed discussion of the common learnings course, it might be well to lay one ghost to rest. From the earlier discussion some of our readers may have been led to believe that we see no value in the standard subjects of the high school. This is not true. We believe that every pupil will have various special interests and/or needs which can best be met through specialized courses. To illustrate, many pupils have vocational needs which can only be met through various types of vocational courses. College preparatory pupils variously require highly systematic courses in science, mathematics, social science, foreign languages, and English which are geared to their needs and higher level of capabilities. Other pupils have non-college preparatory interests in these and other specialized subjects, and so on. Our apparent cavil against the standard subjects is more apparent than real. What we have by inference complained about above is rather the fruitless attempt to make these subjects serve basically important purposes which they were never intended to meet and which they can never adequately fulfill except as the pursuit of the values which they severally typify is abandoned. Clearly, the question is *not* whether we should have the common learnings course *or* specialized subjects. We need *both*.

Let us now become a little more explicit about the common

learnings course. This required offering would be completely prob-lem-centered, and the problems treated would in every instance be real. Although they would necessarily have to be respectably literate in reference to these problems in order to guide youth effectively, neither the teachers nor anybody else would know the final "answers" or "solutions" to any of the problems dealt with.

The "content" of this course would derive from (1) the unre-solved problems variously associated with the effective carrying out of the basic social processes essential for societal survival, and (2) the common real-life personal problems of the youth group in question.

In reference to the first type of "content," the school would obviously have to restrict its choice to those which it believed to be most important, then narrow this selection still further to include only those which the maturity levels of the various grade groups would sanction as sensible to attack. Each category of societal prob-lems to be included should first be broken down into meaningful wholes (parts), and each such meaningful whole problem (part of a more inclusive problem) first assigned to the grade level at which it is sufficiently within the experience of the age group in question to justify its consideration by pupils in that particular grade. Serial consideration at different grade levels should be provided as neces-sity or desirability might warrant.

The second type of "content" should be selected in a similar manner. The commonly experienced real-life problems of the pupils in question should obviously be placed at the various grade levels corresponding to the age groups to whom they first became real. Time limitations would undoubtedly force the school to be selective —obviously, those problems deemed most important should be scheduled for attack in preference to those of less significance in the lives of youth. Serial treatment of these more important problems should be provided to the extent and at the age levels deemed neces-sary or desirable.

In sum, so far as the maturity of the pupils and the time avail-able would permit, all of the meaningful components of each major problem category which should be included in the common learn-ings course would thus be allocated to one or more grade levels.

What we have outlined is simply a common sense plan to guarantee that no important societal or personal problem will be omitted unless ruled out by considerations of lack of time or inadequate pupil maturity, and to insure so far as possible that all problems which are included will be meaningfully treated.

That the common learnings course calls for a new type of teaching means among other things that certain steps must be taken to safeguard the psychic security of the teacher. One essential safeguard is to assure that no subject-matter-expectation club be permitted to hang over his head. The other requisite has to do with instructional materials. To force or even to permit a teacher to embark upon this type of teaching without adequate teaching materials is to court disaster both to the course and to the teacher's emotional health. A resource unit must be constructed (or adopted or adapted if already available) in reference to each problem or problem-cluster selected for inclusion in the course. In the construction of each resource unit, teachers from all broad field areas should participate in defining the behavioral statement of objectives to be striven for, in designing a rich variety of suggested learning experiences geared thereto, and in building a list of fruitful teaching-learning materials.

Because this is a changing world, and because this course is designed to make pupils literate in reference to the more important unresolved problems of such a world, the common learnings course must undergo continuous revision. As societal changes occur and new problems emerge, these must be included. As old problems are resolved, these must be dropped. These changes necessitate the building of new resource units and the abandonment of others. And as the character of the pupil population changes—or as the conditions which the pupils confront change—, new commonly experienced personal problems will emerge and old ones drop out of the picture. Again, new or revised resource units should mirror the changed needs.

We shall conclude with a few words epitomizing the potential significance of the common learnings course. Never in history has so much hinged on the race between education and catastrophe. Seldom, if ever, has education been so out-distanced by its frightful competitor as it now so clearly is. Either those who educate must quickly succeed in creating many types of new mind (new attitudes, beliefs, understandings, skills, and pre-dispositions to behavior) or man will become the victim instead of the master of the urgent problems he now confronts both at home and abroad. In such a context, the common learnings course (already established in embryo form in some schools) may easily prove to be the most important social invention in the history of secondary education to date.

ENCOUNTER:
A Theory of the Curriculum which Affirms the Centrality of the Communities of Discourse

ARTHUR R. KING, JR. AND JOHN A. BROWNELL

In the early 1960's educators renewed their use of the term "discipline" to refer to organized bodies of knowledge. At the same time "structure" of the disciplines gained popularity through Bruner's book, **The Process of Education.** * Though there is no necessary connection between "structure" and "the disciplines" (since it is possible to teach a discipline without teaching its structure and similarly it is possible to teach the structure of something which is not a discipline†),

---

* Jerome S. Bruner, *The Process of Education* (Cambridge, Mass.: Harvard University Press, 1960).

† Jane R. Martin, "The Disciplines and the Curriculum," *Educational Philosophy and Theory* 1 (1969): 23–40.

the last decade has seen the wedding of these two terms into the single term, the "structure of the disciplines." So today when educators speak of "structure" or "disciplines," they imply the complete new term.

King and Brownell in this article propose a curriculum based on the structure of the separate disciplines. Though they refer to Jerome S. Bruner* and Philip Phenix,† two earlier and perhaps better known advocates of a curriculum based on the structure of the disciplines, King and Brownell appear to go further. Bruner (implicitly) and Phenix (explicitly) are committed only to teaching material drawn from the disciplines. They do not state how that material is to be organized but only that it should come from the disciplines. They do not require, as King and Brownell apparently do, that each school subject be a separate discipline.§ Phenix puts his view this way, ". . . it is not to be concluded that the materials of instruction ought necessarily to be organized into separate courses each of which pertains to one of the disciplines. . . . It is possible to use knowledge from the disciplines in connection with studies that cut across several disciplines." ††

It is because of their stronger and hence more challenging position that the King and Brownell proposal is included here. These authors are alert to possible charges of extremism, that is, being placed at one extreme end of the dichotomy identified by Dewey between subject matter and the child. (See the Introduction to this book.) The authors explicitly state that they do not "advocate a return to 'traditional' pedagogy." They go on to say, "On the contrary, we propose a new conception of curriculum which makes the long-standing educational argument between **child-centeredness** and **subject matter** unnecessary and unproductive. The fulfillment of each person's capacity for meanings through encounters with the significant realms of experience is the most humane of educational ideas." //

It is in this light that the reader should compare this King and

---

* Bruner, *The Process of Education.*

† Philip Phenix, *Realms of Meaning* (New York: McGraw-Hill Book Company, 1964).

§ See footnote 2.

†† Phenix, *Realms of Meaning,* p. 319.

// Arthur R. King, Jr. and John A. Brownell, *The Curriculum and the Disciplines of Knowledge* (New York: John Wiley & Sons, Inc., 1966), p. 94.

Brownell article with other articles, Dewey (Chapter 1), Stratemeyer (Chapter 3), Ammons (Chapter 10), and Bellack (Chapter 6).

<del>◇◇◇</del>

We have proposed the *community of discourse** as a theory model for devising a curriculum theory which gives primacy to the claim of intellect. As we now begin to explicate our theory of the curriculum, we shall briefly reopen a line of supporting argument from social and political perspectives for the priority of the claim of intellect in American schools and colleges in this era.

American political and social theory and practice, while not deciding the issue of certain natural inequalities of man—physical and mental—assert the moral, legal, and political equality of persons, and in theory at least their social equality. Furthermore, po-

"Encounter: A Theory of the Curriculum which Affirms the Centrality of the Communities of Discourse" by Arthur R. King, Jr. and John A. Brownell is reprinted with permission from their book *The Curriculum and the Disciplines of Knowledge* (New York: John Wiley & Sons, Inc., 1966). This selection here is from pp. 117–25.

---

* In an earlier part of the book from which this selection is taken the authors deal at length with the "community of discourse." As part of their recapitulation of that chapter the authors write: "We undertake that most dangerous game—the pursuit of isomorphic (an isomorph is something identical with, equal to, alike, or the same as something else in form, shape, or structure) features of the several autonomous disciplines. We find these isomorphic aspects:

A discipline is a community of persons.
A discipline is an expression of human imagination.
A discipline is a domain.
A discipline is a tradition.
A discipline is a syntactical structure—a mode of inquiry.
A discipline is a conceptual structure—a substance.
A discipline is a specialized language or other system of symbols.
A discipline is a heritage of literature and artifacts and a network of communications.
A discipline is a valuative and affective stance.
A discipline is an instructive community." (p. 15) R.T.H., ed.

litical and social theorists have emphasized that schooling provides the common culture of Americans to generations of immigrants.

Deemed essential for good order, public wisdom, and the exercise of the franchise from the earliest days of the Republic, literacy has gained new meaning through the years. It has grown from the ability to read, write, and calculate to include, as well, the possession of extensive knowledge and modes of thought. Clearly, as the complexity of political and social issues increases, the cognitive demand on the citizenry increases. A modern, technological democracy requires intellect.

The rise of urban, industrial society has helped cause schooling to be considered a full-time occupation, first for the child, then for the adolescent, and now, increasingly, for the young adult. Further technological development has tended to eliminate the kind of labor which requires the least schooling and least thoughtful participation of the worker in his job.

Springing from the commitment to the equality of persons, from the theory of American government, and from the influences of urban, industrial characteristics of our society, "equal opportunity for schooling" has grown in meaning to "equal opportunity to engage in the quality curriculum," that curriculum reserved in other times and in other societies for the ruling elite. The "best" curriculum is for all.

The organization and the program of the schools is not yet consonant with the intellectual, social, political, and economic realities of our time. As presently organized, the comprehensive elementary school provides a common or undifferentiated curriculum in a specific number of grades or units of time for all students. However, this curriculum is not a microcosm of the world of knowledge, nor does it provide for students to move as rapidly through the curriculum as they are capable. The secondary school offers a wide collection of studies or a differentiated curriculum in a specific number of units of time. One portion of the studies, college preparatory, reflects some concern with the claim of intellect and is related recognizably to the aspects of the realm of knowledge. Other portions reflect other claims. The college offers a wide array of studies in its curriculum, but requires a high degree of common study in the disciplines of knowledge in lower division. Neither the secondary school or college—with notable exceptions—freely permits advancement as quickly as is possible. The cognitive demands of political and economic life, we submit, require a common program of studies through the secondary level for all students. Because the cognitive domain is made intelligible best by the communities of organized knowledge, the common program of studies concerns the world of knowledge organized into disciplines. In order to meet these demands, schools and colleges, faced with the apparent inequalities of physical and mental talent in the normal population, perforce must escape from the lock-step progression of students on the time-scale. Individual performance in a discipline will not be identifiable by the year in school.

Bringing the schools into closer harmony with the conditions of a modern, industrial, democratic republic will inevitably emphasize the intellectual component of schooling. There is, then, support for the priority of intellect from the present situation of American life.

For many persons these kinds of argument—social, political, occupational—are the only ones that matter, for they are judged "practical." However, we have set forth the primacy of the claim of intellect on the curriculum on additional bases: (1) the symbolic capacity of mankind, including verbal, mathematical, aesthetic, and religious forms; (2) the worth of persons and their freedom, which requires the foresighted envisioning or symbolizing of choices; (3) the functioning organization of mankind's symbolic efforts—the disciplines of knowledge which represent at any one time the realm of intellect in its most learnable and useful form; and (4) the self-correcting critical role of intellect with respect to all other aspects of life. These arguments we believe transcend the conditions of social groups, national boundaries, and a limited view of time.

Whatever the bases for support, we propose the primacy of the intellectual claim on the content of the curriculum as the cornerstone of our theory. As a corollary, the ranking of the other claims will be determined by judgment. These other claims are not treated in this work.

While the school performs many functions, its chief one is curricular. The heart of the general curriculum is the disciplines of knowledge. Below we have set out a scheme for illustrating the functions:

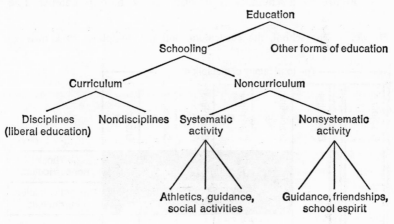

FIGURE 1

We have defined the school as a microcosm of the world of intellect. The curriculum in the disciplines is the heart of such a school. The curricular function is paramount. The nondiscipline curriculum—straightforward occupational, social, and personal training—should not under any circumstances replace an element of the liberal curriculum for any student. Occupational training desirably follows liberal studies and should occur just before the individual's departure from organized schooling. Preferably, occupational training should take place in a program designed for industry or an occupation and carried out in a special setting such as the technical institute, on-the-job-training program, armed services school, or other well-resourced special program. If the school is required by law or other mandate to teach nondisciplined matter in an organized fashion, it should use great ingenuity in locating such training (as driver education, grooming, or personal typing) in after-school hours, on Saturdays, or in summers. The noncurricular functions which are organized and financed by the school should be generally supportive of intellect and culture.

Figure 2 is a schematic representation of these statements. The

FIGURE 2 The school, the curriculum, and the disciplines of knowledge

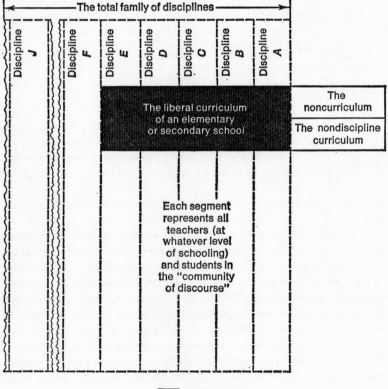

school consists of a purposefully selected set of disciplines from among the total family of disciplines, plus the minor components of nondisciplined studies and the noncurricular functions. The figure suggests that the disciplines are *in* the school, that teachers and students are a working part of the discourse of each discipline.

The figure suggests further that the central issue of any curriculum design is the inclusion/omission of disciplines of knowledge. The theory and mechanism for rendering this decision and for reviewing it in light of alternative elements is one about which little is known, but requires, nevertheless, delineation. We devote Chapters VI and VII to this issue. The second major issue in curriculum theory is that of the responsible programming of the curriculum of a discipline. We delineate the implications of our theory for this issue in Chapter VIII.

THE HEART OF THE MATTER

In Chapter III we set forth *the community of discourse* as a representation of the world of knowledge and described the community's general attributes. We also proposed the community of discourse or discipline of knowledge as a theory model for devising a curriculum theory. We shall now proceed to state the general characteristics of our theory of the curriculum devised from the model.

Specifically, we propose that the curriculum be viewed with respect to several conditions. First, *the communities of discourse or disciplines of knowledge are represented in a school.* They are not "subjects" or "studies" or "content areas" selected *from* the disciplines of knowledge; they are not accretions of haphazardly selected concepts, skills, or understandings; they are not unities of ideas unknown in the widest realm of intellectual endeavor. It is the communities of discourse per se that are in the school. Each discipline brings with it a fabric of skills and values. For example, *reading, writing,* and *speaking* are integral to language—hence they cannot be separated from language study. Such values as integrity, self-control, truthfulness, objectivity, and beauty are exemplified and practiced in one or another form of disciplined inquiry. Because commitments to values, freely given, are the only significant and lasting kind, we do not believe that it is possible to establish specific programs for indoctrination in values. Value theories are central to literature, ethics, aesthetics, and political theory, among others.

The teacher is a veteran of encounters within the community of discourse; he is, and will remain, a member and exemplar of the body of discoursers at some mature level. Most importantly he is a continuing member of the discipline who has reflected on the nature of that discipline, its traditions, its ways of gaining knowledge, its assumptions about what can be known and how it can be known and how its knowledge is warranted. Not all of the community of discoursers will have so reflected, but the teacher must. It is an essential, conscious part of his preparation as a teacher.

The student is a neophyte* in the encounters with the community of discourse; he is, nevertheless, to be considered a member of the community, immature to be sure, but capable of virtually unlimited development. He is learning the ways of gaining knowledge in the discipline, continually reorganizing the principles or concepts which his studies and discoveries have provided, seeking always to gain meaning through the ensemble of fundamental principles that characterize the discipline at this time.

The curriculum can now be defined in that form for which all else has been building. *The liberal curriculum is a planned series of encounters between a student and some selection of communities of discourse.* An encounter is a face-to-face meeting, a personal conflict or contact involving action and reaction. An educational encounter brings the student personally into association— one might almost say communion—with a variety of areas of important thought and discourse. The student must be engaged with

---

* The term *neophyte* is applicable to one, often eager and unsophisticated, newly connected with or entered into a group, society, faith, or pursuit. *Webster's Third International Dictionary, Unabridged,* 1961.

both the process and the product in the sciences and the arts. Only with the practice of judgment and skill in analysis can such encounters be planned; in the school which grants intellect prime claim, planning cannot be eschewed, vagueness cannot be approved.

But planning for discovery is not simple. Each community of discourse in the school is not only exemplified by the teacher, but also through visitors, books, musical organizations, paintings, sculptures, ceramic creations, recordings, radio and television programs and series, programmed learning materials, all chosen as most representative of the discipline. To the highest degree obtainable, then, the curriculum faithfully represents the most significant portions of the realm of knowledge at work, each in its own way.

As used in a restricted sense, the curriculum in a single discipline of knowledge is the complete set of courses in the discipline. Seldom will the complete set capture the growing edge of the discipline, no matter how imaginatively planned, for as we have suggested in Chapters II and III the discipline is a dynamic movement, and discovery will move faster than the ability of any school or college to plan encounters for the young.

We further define *a course as a planned series of encounters with the structure of any single discipline,* typically for an age, grade, ability, or interest group of students. A course will be based on the historic and current nature of the discipline. It will embody a plan for knowing the discipline, that is, for working as a member of the community of discoursers. This plan will be organized around promising points of encounter or contact for the induction of the novice or for maturing the advanced student. The points of encounter will be arranged according to some strategy of knowing, some way of sustaining the encounter which characterizes the experienced practitioners. Periodically these ordered points will be recorded in a concise written statement or syllabus. Based on the syllabus, a logistic support subsystem will be developed so that study questions, books, laboratory equipment, films, records, even buildings suit the requirements for the course. Some member of the body of discoursers in the school will be selected to carry out the planned series of encounters or will produce a substitute syllabus pertinent to the characteristics set forth. From the discipline, as represented in the syllabus, a plan of appraisal will be derived. The teacher, guided by the syllabus, by his own creative interpretations and artistry as a veteran in the discipline, and by the quality of student engagement, will initiate, carry out, and appraise the encounters. The teacher and perhaps others will apply the appraisal system for review and reteaching, for syllabus revision, for revision of teaching styles, and for record purposes. *While the course is an analytically and systematically planned series of encounters, it is expressly incomplete without the teacher and student, without their active involvement in the dialogue and discovery which characterizes all of the practitioners of the discipline wherever they may be.*

Given the communities of discourse in the schools, the teacher as a veteran discourser, the student as one being inducted and developed in each community of intellectual discourse, the curriculum as a planned series of encounters with the communities of intellectual discourse, the course as a system of planned encounters with a particular discipline, the school is thereby redefined. This curriculum theory compels thought about the nature of the school. A school is not a building. It is not a bureaucracy. It is not an attendance center. It is not an extension of an administrator's mind or his philosophy nor the expression of the local citizenry. To use a Chaucerian line, *the school is a "company of sundry folk."* In essence the company is an organically related composite of the communities of intellectual discourse, although in practice many American schools and colleges have faculty in applied fields or services. But why call it a company? What characteristics does that metaphor suggest which "community of scholars" or "community of learning" or "commonwealth of learning" or any of the numerous other suggestions do not? We offer these.

The learned company is a band or group of persons with a mission; its mission is to inquire after truth, to communicate what has been discovered in order to eradicate ignorance, to develop latent capacities for intellectual adventure, and to take some part in the making of persons. It has an imperative. From its mission it gains a sense of unity.

By calling attention to the "sundry folk," we mean to emphasize the pluralism of knowledge, the philosophic differences, the richness and diversity of the school faculty and student body, with the necessary dialogue, debate, and tension among them as essential to their well-being. This company is a microcosm of intellectual life established and maintained in a local community. The idea of a school as a "company," we believe, is as pertinent to the elementary and secondary schools as to higher education.

The company makes demands on its members, that is, it disciplines its members under a system of authority. The system of authority is constantly reviewed by its members, and it is tied in with other democratic systems of warranted authority.

The company therefore demands a commitment from its members: to accept the mission and traditions of the band, to extend and welcome criticism among members. A commitment is a belief *in* something, not a belief *that* something is. To the faculty, the commitment requires involvement, an acceptance of responsibility to engage in dialogue and tension with good will and forcefulness with peers; to remain current with the particular body of discoursers of which one is a member; to respect one's formative influence on students; to participate in decision making in the larger arena of curriculum decisions; and to undertake the necessary and sometimes onerous tasks associated with teaching.

The learned company has a tradition of essential equality among its adult members. One part is freedom for any member to make a significant contribution. Another part is that the young are gradually inducted into both the disciplines and the company to the point where they may make important contributions as equals as quickly as possible. Differentiation of function among faculty and administration does not mean inequality.

The company of learning respects the dual commitment between membership in a discipline and membership in a school faculty. Members of a faculty should never be expected to give up membership in a particular discipline in order to achieve or retain a position on the faculty of a school.

The presence of a discipline in a certain school is not fully permanent, for new disciplines are added and some are dropped. Decisions on adding and dropping are best made by the company (faculty and administration) and influenced partially by elements outside the school operating through legal channels.

In its unremitting examination, analysis, and criticism of its own performance and function, as well as the state's and society's, the company requires academic freedom and academic due process.

The learned company provides fellowship of kindred souls, producing morale, power, pleasure, and a noticeable spirit of the school. It recruits students to the life of the mind, to the search for truth, to the creation and enjoyment of the beautiful.

IMPLICATIONS OF THE THEORY

We are proposing that the school be developed, organized, and operated in harmony with the requirements of the curriculum. We believe that the programming of the curriculum, the deriving of a structure for school organization, and the operating of a school should be consistent with the theory of curriculum and give it all possible support. At this stage we merely wish to mention some of the elements which must be considered: school administration, teaching, teacher education, organization for curricular change, school organization, student activities, instructional materials, and course advisement. Detailed consideration of these points is in the remainder of this book.

WHAT KNOWLEDGE IS OF MOST WORTH?

ARNO A. BELLACK

In tackling again Spencer's question of the 19th century, "What Knowledge Is of Most Worth?", Arno Bellack relies on current work in England and the U.S.A. as well as on the older work of the progressives in the three decades following World War I. It is his awareness of the problems associated with the teaching of the disciplines and also those associated with the teaching of youth's problems that leads Bellack to a proposal encompassing selected elements of both.

Bellack's contention that the broad fields are preferable to the separate disciplines for purposes of curriculum planning recalls the work of Alvin M. Weinberg in an article in **Science** magazine, August

6, 1965.* It is well to point out that Weinberg, a natural scientist and director of the Oak Ridge National Laboratory in Tennessee, compliments Bellack whose own strength lies in the social science field. Weinberg, in discussing the relationship between the university and society, claims that the tendency "toward purity and fragmentation as opposed to application and interdisciplinarity" that curriculum reform projects acquired from the university scholars associated with them, are dangerous for the projects and society. Hence, for pregraduate work (all education through high school and college, prior to graduate school) Weinberg supports a broad approach to curriculum where interdisciplinary connections are emphasized.

The reader should also carefully note Bellack's points based on the work of the two Britons, Peterson and Toulmin. Peterson's "modes of thought" and Toulmin's "onlooker's language" offer two concepts generally not associated with curriculum planning yet having importance for teaching, according to Bellack.

The reader should compare Bellack with King and Brownell (Chapter 5) in regard to the treatment of the disciplines and with Hand (Chapter 4) and Metcalf and Hunt (Chapter 8) in regard to the treatment of the problems of youth. The points raised by Wise (Chapter 7) in rejection of other curriculum proposals and those by Berman (Chapter 11) regarding the priority of processes over the disciplines deserve close attention in light of Bellack's claims.

◇◇

During the current period of curriculum reform, most of the debate hinges on an old and familiar question: "What shall the schools teach?" This is a perennial question that apparently every generation has to solve over again for itself in the light of changing conditions and changing needs. And it is a question that can be

"What Knowledge Is of Most Worth?" by Arno A. Bellack is reprinted with permission from *The High School Journal*, 48 (February, 1965): 318–32.

* Alvin M. Weinberg, "But Is the Teacher Also a Citizen?" *Science* 149, No. 3684 (August 6, 1965): 601–6.

answered only by reference to one's view of the nature of knowledge, for by universal agreement knowledge is the stock-in-trade of the school.

It is well to remind ourselves that the current debates about knowledge and the curriculum are not over the question of whether knowledge is relevant to the school's task. Although there are different views as to what knowledge should be taught and how it is to be taught, most educators would agree that knowledge is one of the primary responsibilities of the school. Few would deny that the fields of organized inquiry are significant aspects of our culture which the school is uniquely equipped to introduce to students. No other agency or institution in our society has the personnel or other resources to perform this function effectively. Unless students become acquainted with these important facets of our culture in school it is doubtful that they will learn about them elsewhere, at least not so well.

It is important to stress this at the outset, for today one frequently hears the view expressed that educationists responsible for planning the curriculum of the elementary and secondary schools have only recently, and belatedly, come to recognize that knowledge is a significant factor in teaching and in preparation for teaching. A brief glance at the historical development of the school curriculum should help to set the record straight on this score. Throughout our history, most elementary and secondary programs have been organized around the time-honored school subjects, even during the heyday of progressivism in the decades prior to World War II. The progressives too had a place for knowledge in their scheme of things: the curriculum was to be organized around personal and social problems, and the academic disciplines were to serve as resources in dealing with these problems. Emphasis was on the *practical* ordering of knowledge with reference to problems to be solved. It was this central idea that attracted the sympathies of many educators who questioned the ability of the traditional school to provide an effective way of preparing students to face the increasingly complex problems of modern living.

Contemporary efforts to redefine the role of knowledge in the curriculum place emphasis on the *logical* order inherent in knowledge itself, on the structure of concepts and principles of inquiry that characterize the various fields of learning. Whereas formerly factual and descriptive content was stressed, now the emphasis is on basic concepts and methods scholars use as intellectual tools to analyze and order their data.

Several claims are made for teaching the fundamental structures of the disciplines, two of which are of central importance and worth considering here. The first is that understanding of fundamental ideas is the main road to adequate transfer of training. Professor Bruner, who is largely responsible for introducing the concept of structure into educational discourse, observes that

> knowledge is a model we construct to give meaning and structure to regularities in experience. The organizing ideas of any body of knowledge are inventions for rendering experience economical and connected. We invent concepts such as force in physics, the bond in chemistry, motives in psychology, style in literature as means to the end of comprehension. . . . The power of great organizing concepts is in large part that they permit us to understand and sometimes to predict or change the world in which we live. But their power lies also in the fact that ideas provide instruments for experience.

Therefore, he contends, "the structure of knowledge—its connectedness and its derivations that make one idea follow another—is the proper emphasis in education." [1]

The second important claim for emphasis on structure is that by constantly re-examining material taught in the schools for its fundamental patterns of organization, the schools will be able to narrow the gap between "advanced" knowledge and "elementary" knowledge. Since scholars at the forefront of their disciplines are able to make the greatest contribution to the substantive reorganization of their fields, current curriculum projects place great em-

---

[1] Jerome S. Bruner, *On Knowing*. (Cambridge, Massachusetts, Harvard University Press, 1962), p. 120.

phasis on the participation of university researchers in continuing revision of the program of studies. Scholars in the various disciplines and their professional organizations have in recent years made proposals for revamping the curriculum in elementary and secondary schools—first in mathematics, physics, chemistry, and biology; then in English; and recently and belatedly in economics, geography, anthropology, and history.

The focus of attention in each of these projects is an individual discipline. Little or no attention is given to the relationships of the individual fields to each other or to the program of studies within which they must find their place. National committees in the fields of chemistry, physics, and biology have proceeded independently of each other. The projects in economics, geography, and anthropology are unrelated to one another or to the other social sciences. Only in mathematics has there been a disposition to view the field as a whole, but this is a reflection of developments within the discipline of mathematics at the highest levels of scholarship.

The situation developing in the elementary and secondary schools thus begins to reflect, at least to some degree, the state of affairs in the universities with respect to the development and organization of knowledge, which Professor John Randall has described in this way:

> As reflected in the microcosm of the modern university, the world of knowledge has today become radically plural. It is a world of many different knowledges, pursued in varied ways to diverse ends. These many inquiries are normally carried on with little thought for their relation to each other. The student of John Donne's poetry, the student of the structure of the atom—each gives little enough attention to what the others are doing, and none at all to any total picture of anything. Each has his own goals, his own methods, his own language for talking about what he is doing and what he has discovered. Each seems happiest when left to his own devices, glad indeed if he can keep others from treading on his toes. Each is convinced that what he himself is doing is worth while. But none has too much respect for the others, though he is willing enough to tolerate them. They have all little understanding of each other's pursuits—

what they are trying to do, how they are are doing it, and what they really mean when they talk about it.[2]

I emphasize this pluralism in the academic world not to deplore it, but to call attention to the problem that it presents for those who are concerned with the organization of the entire curriculum. For the curriculum builder is concerned not only with the structures of the individual disciplines, but also with the structure of the instructional program within which the fields of knowledge find their place. The problem can be very simply stated, if not easily solved: What general structure of the curriculum can be developed so that autonomy of the parts does not result in anarchy in the program as a whole? This is one of two questions I propose to discuss briefly.

The second question grows out of the proposal that students be introduced to the ways of thinking associated with the various disciplines in such fashion that they in fact become physicists, chemists, or economists. Professor Bruner puts it this way:

> What a scientist does at his desk or in his laboratory, what a literary critic does in reading a poem, are of the same order as what anybody else does when he is engaged in like activities—if he is to achieve understanding. The difference is in degree, not in kind. The schoolboy learning physics is a physicist.[3]

I take it this does not mean that the goal of general education is to train all students as specialists in mathematics, geography, history, or whatever other subjects they might study. Rather, the goal is to make available to students the intellectual and aesthetic resources of their culture in such a way that they become guides for intelligent action and help students create meaning and order

---

[2] John H. Randall, Jr., "The World to be Unified," in Lewis Leary, ed., *The Unity of Knowledge.* (Garden City, New York, Doubleday and Company, 1955), p. 63.
[3] Jerome S. Bruner, *The Process of Education.* (Cambridge, Harvard University Press, 1960), p. 14.

out of the world in which they find themselves. Professor Bestor, who scarcely qualifies as an advocate of education for life adjustment, has made this same point:

> The modern scientist or the modern scholar knows the delight of intellectual endeavor for its own sake, and he rightly resents the undervaluing of this motive. But when all is said and done he knows that the principal value to society of a man's cultivating the power of abstract thought is that he is thereby enabled to deal more effectively with the insistent problems of modern life. . . . The basic argument for the intellectual disciplines in education is not that they lift a man's spirits above the world, but that they equip his mind to enter the world and perform its tasks.[4]

How is this widely accepted objective to be realized? Is the ability to relate what is learned in school to the world of human affairs to come as an inevitable by-product of the study of the disciplines, or must teachers give explicit attention to helping students see the relevance of such study for their own lives as individuals, citizens, and workers? This is the second issue I propose to discuss briefly.

I. KNOWLEDGE AND THE STRUCTURE OF THE CURRICULUM

When we look beyond the structures of the disciplines and ask about the structure of the curriculum within which the various fields of study take their place, we face a problem of the greatest complexity. What knowledge from the vast array of intellectual resources shall the schools teach? The accumulated and ever-growing knowledge in all fields has reached such proportions that comprehensive grasp of the total range of knowledge is out of the ques-

---

[4] Arthur Bestor, *Educational Wastelands.* (Urbana, University of Illinois Press, 1953), p. 15.

tion for any one individual. The question raised by Spencer a hundred years ago, "What knowledge is of most worth?" is even more relevant today than it was in his time. Given the limited time and capacity of the school, what shall the schools teach to secure results that can be generalized beyond the immediate situations in which the learning takes place?

According to long and honorable tradition, knowledge is grouped for pedagogical purposes in four major categories—the natural sciences, the social sciences, mathematics, and the humanities (the latter an omnibus term that includes art, literature, philosophy, and music). These broad groupings of organized disciplines are generally recognized as basic cultural interests of our society which constitute both the resources and the obligations of the schools. Each major field represents distinctive methods and conceptual schemes in which the world and man are viewed from quite different vantage points. Instruction in these areas has as its primary goal equipping students with key concepts and methods that inform and sustain intelligent choice in human affairs.

Although the four major areas of knowledge are generally recognized as important components of the curriculum, they are not currently used as the context or framework for curriculum building. Instead, as we have already noted, recent curriculum projects have focused attention on individual disciplines without concern for their relationships to allied fields. Thus the economists, the geographers, and the anthropologists have proceeded independently of each other, as have the biologists, chemists, and physicists. To be sure, economists suggest ways in which economic ideas can be taught in history; and anthropologists show how some of their generalizations can be woven into courses in geography. This is all to the good; it even seems to suggest that integration of a limited variety might be appropriate for teaching purposes. But scant attention is given to building a curriculum design within which the individual fields might find their place.

It is my contention that this approach has certain inherent shortcomings and that we would do well to shift the context for curriculum planning from the individual disciplines, as is now the vogue, to the broad groupings of knowledge represented by the natural sciences, the social sciences, mathematics, and the humanities. Let us briefly consider some of the problems involved in curriculum building in the social sciences to show why this proposed shift is desirable and necessary.

The social sciences—economics, social psychology, political science, sociology, anthropology, geography, and history—are all seeking explanations of the same phenomenon, man's social life. This common goal is what makes it reasonable to group them together as the *social* sciences. All of them have grown out of man's attempt to interpret, understand, and control the social environment. But each field formulates its own questions about this subject matter and develops its own system of concepts to guide its research. The economist is preoccupied with the concept of scarcity, the political scientist with the concepts of power and authority, the anthropologist with the notion of culture, and the sociologist with social functions and social systems. Each science is thus abstract, dealing with only certain facets of actual social relationships and institutions—facets that do not permit of physical separation, but only of analytical separation.

Man's social life as it is actually lived is therefore far more complex than the limited image of it reflected in the concepts and generalizations of any one of the social disciplines. It follows then, as Professor Kingsley Davis has suggested, that "in so far as the prediction of actual events is concerned, the various social sciences are mutually interdependent, because only by combining their various points of view can anything approaching a complete anticipation of future occurrences be achieved." [5] Policies that are proposed and actions that are taken to deal with problems in social affairs are of necessity interdisciplinary, for concrete social reality is not mirrored in the findings of any one discipline.

Now this is a matter of central importance to those whose job it is to plan and organize the social studies curriculum. To focus

---

[5] *Human Society.* (New York, The Macmillan Company, 1948), p. 8.

exclusive attention on certain aspects of the social world as seen through the eyes of one or two of the social sciences is to give students a myopic vision of man's social behavior and his institutions. To shape children's conceptions of the social world through exclusive emphasis on the language of the economist, for example, to the exclusion of the language of the sociologist, political scientist, anthropologist, and historian is to determine that they shall interpret human affairs principally in terms that the economist uses to view reality—in terms of supply, demand, scarcity, production, and consumption.

Students must be helped to see the limitations as well as the uses of a single discipline in interpreting events as they actually occur. And for anything approaching a comprehensive view of man's functioning in society, the specialized perspectives of all the social sciences are needed. Curriculum builders in the social studies have the enormously difficult job of providing a place in their programs for all the social sciences, each of which contributes its distinctive perspective on human institutions and human behavior.

It is clear that such a program can be developed only on the basis of collaboration among the various social sciences. Such collaboration does not presuppose a "unified social science" as the basis for planning the elementary and secondary school curriculum. Quite the opposite is the case. For the social disciplines today are characterized by a plurality of methods and conceptual schemes developed by social scientists to deal with problems within their individual spheres. Instead of a unity of method or a single universe of discourse, we find a vast confederation of separate areas of study. Modes of thinking and analysis differ from field to field, and even from problem to problem within the same field. In time, a Bacon of the sciences that bear on the social and cultural behavior of man may emerge, but that time is not yet.

At the same time, in spite of increasing specialization and internal differentiation, there are interconnections among the social sciences that curriculum planning for the schools should take into account. For example, the various social sciences borrow rather handily from each other when it comes to both concepts and methods. Historians make use of concepts from all the other social sciences. Political scientists interested in political socialization get their methods from behavioral scientists and seem in many respects more closely related to sociologists and social psychologists than to fellow political scientists. Certain anthropologists have utilized the Freudian view of human development in analyzing patterns of various cultures. Geographers make extensive use of the perspectives of history and concepts developed by all the behavioral sciences.

Furthermore, we find not only interchange of concepts and methods but growing collaboration among specialists. For example, studies of the nature and function of "authority" are now undertaken jointly by political scientists and sociologists; and there have been recent studies conducted by economists in collaboration with anthropologists to determine whether certain economic theories hold for different types of economic systems. The convergence of social scientists upon the same problems has given rise to what Professor Robert Merton calls "interdisciplines" such as social biology, political sociology, and sociological history.

The picture that emerges from this cursory review of the current state of affairs in the social sciences is one of great diversity. Given this mosaic of disciplines and interdisciplines, each characterized by multiple conceptual schemes and methods, the curriculum builder is faced with the problem of developing structures for teaching that relate the social sciences to each other in meaningful ways and avoid undue fragmentation of knowledge.

What has been said about the social sciences applies in principle to the natural sciences, mathematics, and the humanities. The significant point is that there is a need for a broader context for curriculum planning than the separate disciplines, and the broad fields of knowledge furnish a useful framework for this purpose. I am not calling for indiscriminate scrambling of superficial knowledge. Indeed, at this point we would do well to suspend judgment as to when in the school program teaching should be organized around the individual disciplines, and when around the broad groupings of the disciplines. In all likelihood, different patterns of organization will be found to be appropriate for different levels of the school program. Dewey's notion of the "progressive organization of knowledge," long ignored by most of his interpreters, might serve as a guiding hypothesis in planning the sequence of the program through the elementary and secondary school years.

In sum, scholars in the natural sciences, the social sciences, mathematics, and the humanities should now be invited to join in the search for new structures for teaching—structures that respect the integrity of the individual fields and at the same time help these fields find their place in a pattern of studies that provides a substantial measure of coherence and relatedness for the program as a whole.

But there is not only the question of relationship among disciplines that deal with similar problems or phenomena, but also the question of the relationships among the broad areas of knowledge— the sciences and mathematics on the one hand, and the humanities on the other. The growing separation and lack of effective communication between the arts and sciences have been widely noted and greatly deplored. C. P. Snow's analysis of this situation in terms of the two cultures of the literary intellectuals and the scientists is well known to all of us. That this state of affairs should somehow be remedied is the theme of many earnest discussions. The upshot of the discussion is usually that there is one way out of all this: it is, as Snow suggests, by rethinking our education.

But how shall the school go about bridging the gulf between the literary and aesthetic and the scientific studies? It seems reasonable to inquire first of all if human knowledge in its many dimensions forms a recognized unity within which the fields of inquiry and creativity fall neatly into place. Is there a sense in which all knowledge is one, with the arts and the sciences having a place in a unity of fundamental principles or basic methods of inquiry?

The progressives, taking their cue from Dewey, found for themselves such a unity in the "scientific method" (or the "method of intelligence," as it was frequently labeled) that was assumed to characterize all types of rational, intelligent activity in academic pursuits and in artistic and practical affairs as well. The problem-solving method came to be viewed as the basic ingredient in programs of general education.

But by no means is there agreement among scientists that there is a single all-encompassing set of procedures, even in the natural sciences, as assumed by those who talk about *the* scientific method. There seems to be little warrant for assuming that there is one overarching method sufficiently flexible and inclusive to deal with problems in the various scientific fields, to say nothing of the arts, crafts, and applied areas. Indeed, as we have already noted, the intellectual world today is characterized by a plurality of methods and conceptual schemes developed by the disciplines to deal with problems within their individual spheres. Analysis of the various disciplines reveals a wide range of organizations and intellectual methods associated with them. Instead of a unity of method or a single universe of discourse, we are confronted with a vast confederation of separate areas of study. Modes of analysis differ from field to field, and even from problem to problem within the same field.

The heterogeneous character of the intellectual resources that are a part of the culture is a fact of major significance for the curriculum builder. We would do well frankly to recognize this and make a place in our programs for the variety of logical orders that characterize the fields of knowledge on which we draw in building the curriculum.

But what then of the relationships among the various fields of creativity and inquiry? Is it perhaps possible, in spite of the variety of logical orders characteristic of knowledge in its various branches, to identify the principal kinds of cognitive operations or modes of thinking that characterize man's intellectual activities?

A proposal to facilitate students' insight into relationships among the various fields of knowledge by introducing them to the "principal modes of intellectual activity" comes from Professor Peterson of Oxford University. In making suggestions for the reform of secondary education in Britain, Peterson urges educators to stop thinking of general education in terms of "general knowledge":

> It is not a sign that a man lacks general education if he does not know the date of The Treaty of Utrecht, the latitude of Singapore, the formula for nitro-glycerine or the author of the Four Quartets. It does denote a lack of general education if he cares nothing for any of the arts, confuses a moral judgment with an aesthetic judgment, interprets the actions of Asian political leaders in terms of nineteenth century English parliamentarianism or believes that the existence of God has been scientifically disproved.[6]

Peterson urges therefore that the British secondary schools devise programs of general education not in terms of wide general knowledge, but in terms of development in the main modes of intellectual activity, of which he identifies four: the logical (or the analytic), the empirical, the moral, the aesthetic. These different modes of thought are associated with different uses of language. For example, the empirical mode has to do with statements about the world based on our experience of it. The analytic mode has to do with statements that do not describe the world of fact, but rather tell us how the meanings of symbols are related to one another logically. (A definition is a special case of analytic sentences.) The moral and the aesthetic modes are concerned with statements of preferences, evaluations, and judgments of the good and the evil, the beautiful and the ugly, the desirable and the undesirable.

Any one discipline gives opportunity for the development of more than one mode of thought, and each mode can be developed through more than one of the disciplines. For example, literature can contribute to the development of both moral and aesthetic judgment. Mathematics and philosophy both contribute to the development of the analytic mode. History has probably the widest range of any discipline, for the historian employs all four modes in

---

[6] Oxford University Department of Education, *Arts and Sciences Sides in the Sixth Form.* (Abingdon-Berkshire, The Abbey Press, 1960), p. 13.

constructing his comprehensive interpretation of what happened in the past.

If students are to gain understanding of the similarities and differences among the fields of knowledge, the different modes of mental activity must be made explicit to them:

> They must have time and guidance in which to see that what is a proof in the Mathematics they pursue on Tuesday is not the same kind of thing as a proof in History, which follows on Wednesday; that the truth of George Eliot or Joseph Conrad is not the same thing as the truths of Mendel or Max Plank; and yet that there are similarities as well as differences.[7]

Peterson accordingly suggests that in addition to giving attention to these varying modes of thought in the subject fields, the secondary program include a special course in which these ways of thinking are the object of study. One important aspect of such teaching has to do with ways in which these modes of thought are verified. Verification is particularly significant in that it is the guide to meaning of the various types of thought. For example, empirical statements are verified by tests conducted in terms of experience, whereas moral statements are verified by reference to criteria or principles of judgment. On the other hand, analytic statements depend for their truth on an agreed upon set of rules, and follow logically from accepted definitions.

Thus far I have suggested that in structuring the curriculum with due regard for the relationships among the fields of knowledge we view knowledge from two complementary perspectives. In the first, emphasis is on the conceptual schemes and methods of inquiry associated with the broad fields of knowledge, the natural sciences, the social sciences, mathematics, and the humanities. In the second, attention is focused on modes of thought—the analytic, the empirical, the aesthetic, and the moral—that transcend the boundaries of the individual fields. These two views thus represent mutually

---

[7] *Ibid.,* p. 18.

reinforcing conceptions of knowledge that serve well as the basis for curriculum planning.

Professor Toulmin has coined two terms that might be helpful in clarifying the relationships between these two views of knowledge. He distinguishes between "participant's language" and "onlooker's language." [8] Participant's language is the language used by members of a professional group or discipline as they carry on their work in their specialized field. Hence we talk today about the language of science, the language of psychology, the language of mathemetics, and even the language of education. In the context of our discussion, participant's language has to do with the language system that are the distinguishing characteristics of the various disciplined areas of study such as the sciences, mathematics, and the humanities.

Now if we want to examine or talk about the language we use in any one of these fields, we must use another level of discourse. We must, in Toulmin's terms, use onlooker's language. For example, it was suggested that students need help in understanding that a proof in mathematics is not the same as a proof in science or that the "truth" of a scientist is not the same as the "truth" of the poet or novelist. To make these comparisons and contrasts we need a language system that enables us to look at these various areas of study from the outside, as it were. The principal modes of thought—the analytic, the empirical, the moral, and the aesthetic—furnish us with language tools that are useful for this purpose. Hence their importance in teaching.

In view of the significance of knowledge in our lives today, it seems reasonable to suggest that knowledge itself should become an object of study in the schools. At what points in their educational career students are able to carry on such study with understanding is an empirical question, certainly not answerable in the abstract. High schools might experiment with courses similar to the one suggested by Mr. Peterson for British schools. Already there are

---

[8] S. Toulmin, *Philosophy of Science*. (London, Hutchinson University Library, 1953), p. 13.

available in Britain excellent teaching materials prepared specifically for the kind of teaching here envisaged.[9]

II. RELATIONSHIPS OF KNOWLEDGE TO HUMAN AFFAIRS

That the schools ought to provide students with the means for intelligent action is not a new or controversial idea. When, however, it comes to deciding what to teach and how to teach to accomplish this goal, we find marked differences of opinion.

Is it sufficient in general education, for example, to have students learn how to think like physicists, historians, or economists? I think not. For the economist *as* economist (to mention just one field) is in no position to prescribe courses of action regarding the host of public policy issues we face, and questions of public policy and decision loom large in general education. To be sure, economics does provide us with a body of theory that is essential in examining the probable consequences of alternative economic policies, and a good many of these analytical tools ought to become part of the intellectual equipment of all students. Economists are able to tell us what the probable consequences will be if the supply of money is increased, or if the interest rates are lowered; but they cannot *as* economists tell us whether we ought to take either of these two courses of action. Decisions regarding these alternative courses of action involve technical economic analysis and weighing of values.

It is therefore clear that both values and economic theory are involved in deciding courses of action in economic affairs, and both must find their place in social studies teaching. Here the different modes of thought come prominently into play. Technical economic analysis involves the empirical mode of thinking (that is, it is concerned with matters of fact and theory), while considering alterna-

---

[9] See, for example, the following: E. R. Emmet, *The Use of Reason.* (London, Longmans, Green and Company, Ltd., 1960.) John Wilson, *Language and the Pursuit of Truth.* (London, Cambridge University Press, 1958.) R. W. Young, *Lines of Thought.* (London, Oxford University Press, 1958.)

tive values involves the moral mode (that is, it is concerned with criteria of what is desirable or undesirable). The teacher's job is to help students learn to make these necessary distinctions, so that they recognize when questions of fact and analysis are under consideration and when questions of value are at stake.[10] This would of course hold as well for instruction in fields of study other than economics.

Thus far we have been talking about problems associated with a single field. But problems in the world of human affairs do not come neatly labeled "historical," "economic," or "political." They come as decisions to be made and force us to call upon all we know and make us wish we knew more. It was concern for broad cultural and moral questions that go beyond the boundaries of any one discipline that led the progressives to urge that students have the opportunity to deal with them in all their complexity. They proposed a new curriculum, one centered on the problems of youth and broad social issues and drawing upon the academic disciplines as they become relevant to the problems under study. This idea became the hallmark of progressivism in curriculum building. It gained wide acceptance among educators and found expression in many influential statements of policy and opinion during the 1920's, '30's and '40's. Attempted applications of this viewpoint were made in courses labeled core, common learnings, and the like.

Difficulties in this approach soon became apparent, not the least of which was the students' lack of first-hand acquaintance with the disciplines that were the source of the concepts and ideas essential to structuring problems under study. Without adequate understanding of the various fields of knowledge, students had no way of knowing which fields were relevant to problems of concern to them. Indeed, without knowledge of the organized fields it was difficult for them to ask the kinds of questions about their problems that the various disciplines could help them answer.

---

[10] See *Economic Education in the Schools*. Report of the National Task Force on Economic Education. (New York, Committee for Economic Development, 1961.)

Giving students an opportunity to grapple with broad social and cultural problems was basically a promising innovation. But at the same time one is forced to recognize that problem solving on such a broad base cannot be pursued successfully without growing understanding of the fields of knowledge on which the problem solver must draw.

Recognizing then the value in systematic study of the fields of knowledge and the importance of developing competence in dealing with problems and issues that are broader than those of any one field, the question arises of why opportunities for both types of activities should not be included in the program of all students. One might envision a general education program that would include basic instruction in the major fields defined earlier in this paper (the natural sciences, the social sciences, mathematics, and the humanities), together with a coordinating seminar in which students deal with problems "in the round" and in which special effort is made to show the intimate relationships between the fields of study as concepts from those fields are brought to bear on these problems. Such a seminar would also furnish excellent opportunities to help students become aware of the different modes of thought and various types of language usage involved in dealing with problematic situations and the necessity for making clear distinctions among them.

This is not a new proposal. I am here dusting off an old idea first set forth in the 1956 ASCD Yearbook, *What Shall the High Schools Teach?* [11] Along similar lines, Professor Schwab, at the Disciplines Seminar convened by the Project on Instruction of the National Education Association, proposed a plan for elementary and secondary schools that would reconcile the demands of the disciplines and the needs of our culture and society by considering the curriculum at each level of school as consisting of two parts.[12]

---

[11] Association for Supervision and Curriculum Development. 1956 Yearbook, *What Shall the High Schools Teach?* Chapter IV.

[12] *The Scholars Look at the Schools.* National Education Association, Project on Instruction, The Association, 1962, pp. 51–52.

One part, to be called the nuclear curriculum, would contain materials from the disciplines, selected to fulfill those objectives of education which are determined primarily by the needs of the developing child and the aims imposed by our culture and society. Such materials would be taught, wherever possible, within the frame of the discipline from which they were taken. But where the exigencies of time, of learning competence, or other need required it, these materials would be freely removed from their theoretical or disciplinary context and put into the context of unquestioned principles designed for use.

The second, or cortical, component of the curriculum would be chosen by contrary and complementary principles. It would consist of materials chosen specifically because they are representive of the major disciplines. Such materials would display the more important conceptual frames of each discipline, its techniques of discovery and verification, and the variety of problems to which it addresses itself. Where alternatives existed, preferred materials would be those which also served present and recognized individual-social needs. But the criterion of representativeness of the discipline would be paramount.

Let it be recognized that the difficulties involved in developing programs of general education for high schools that make a place both for the organized fields of knowledge and for problem-solving core courses or coordinating seminars are almost overwhelming. Perhaps the greatest difficulty is that such programs will require the collaboration of specialists in the various disciplines, in learning theory and in teaching. Now one characteristic shared by all specialists is their tendency to view their individual bailiwicks as the center of the universe. Only as specialists in the various fields of knowledge, in learning theory and in teaching develop commitment to a new center of professional concern—the curriculum of the school—will we be able to build programs of general education in our high schools that reflect the best in scholarship, in learning and in teaching.

7

INTEGRATIVE EDUCATION
FOR A DIS-INTEGRATED WORLD

GENE WISE

At the beginning of this article Gene Wise in 1966 specifically delimited his ideas to the college undergraduate curriculum. He did so because of his work at the time at Raymond College of the University of the Pacific. In personal communication about this article Wise recently answered two questions raised by the editor: (1) Do you still hold the views you advocated in 1966? and (2) Do you also propose this curriculum for pre-college students? His answer to both was an emphatic "yes" since he believes that his claims apply to education in general and not only to the specific college undergraduate program. This is important for the reader to keep in mind.

Before presenting his own existentially oriented curriculum focusing on integration, Wise launches into a vigorous attack on the separate disciplines approach and also the interdisciplinary approach often advocated as alternatives for avoiding premature specialization. For this reason it is well to read this section by Wise in light of the points made by King and Brownell (Chapter 5), Bellack (Chapter 6), Hand (Chapter 4), and Metcalf and Hunt (Chapter 8).

In his efforts to get to Wise's main section on an integrated curriculum the reader should not skip lightly over one particular sentence: "Because it is necessarily preparation, and preparation in a world of fundamental intellectual revolutions, education should be essentially methodological rather than substantive." Is Wise correct? In answering this question the reader should consider the points on processes made by Berman (Chapter 11), Ammons (Chapter 10), and Kilpatrick (Chapter 2).

<><><><><><><><><><><><><><><><><><><><><><><><><><><><><><><><><>

To call ours "the age of anxiety" is to echo what is by now a truism. Two world wars and a cold war, world-wide depression and the advent of terror and totalitarianism in east and west, the growth of impersonal bureaucracies throughout the world—continuously we hear that such phenomena threaten our civilization's historic faith in man's potential. Some have called the contemporary world post-Christian. It might also be termed post-Modern, for the great consensus of progressive rationalism characterizing the epoch beginning in the Renaissance and extending to World War II seems to be disintegrating.

The fact of disintegration is inescapable. To deny this is to deny the past fifty years of world history, to nurture a desperate wish which may be comforting in its simplicity but which is irrelevant to the vital concerns of these post-Modern years.

But the obvious truth of disintegration should not blind us to its complexity and heuristic potential. Just as we are now experiencing the painful responsibilities attending that panacea of the

"Integrative Education for a Dis-integrated World" by Gene Wise is reprinted with permission from *Teachers College Record*, 67 (March, 1966): 391–401.

Modern world called Progress, so we may also discover the riches associated with the bugbear of the post-Modern world—Anxiety.

What some sociologists have labelled "the end of ideology" (*1, 12*) may signal the demise of total commitments by "true believers," secular as well as sacred. But ideology need not be replaced by anomie as the dominant intellectual temper. For any situation generating existential anxiety is multi-dimensional: Anxiety may result from a critical challenge to deeply-held faiths, but it may also emerge where opportunities are so numerous that the individual can find no stable resting place on which to lodge his identity.

Expanding potential in a progressively open world—this as much as the above-listed historical tendencies have sharpened contemporary man's anxiety about himself. For when there is so much to do and so many different ways to think and judge, the human dilemma becomes as vexing as that of the proverbial child before the Christmas tree.

CONSEQUENCES OF A DILEMMA

This dilemma has affected several different aspects of life and thought in America today. It may be detected in the rebelliousness and vain quest for purpose in our most intelligent youth, in the strident whine of treason and betrayal heard from a highly successful and upwardly-mobile segment of our middle class (*2*), in the general restlessness of our affluent society, and in a host of other areas where opportunity has seemed paradoxically to generate bitterness and despair rather than excitement and activity. In the present essay, I am concerned with only one large area of the dilemma's impact—with American higher education and, more specifically, with suggesting how it may have released forces by which the undergraduate curriculum may be regenerated with vitality and relevance.*

---

* See the introduction to this article for Wise's expansion on his concern here only with the undergraduate curriculum. R.T.H., ed.

College educators, I believe, have not reflected seriously enough upon the fragmenting effects of a liberal arts curriculum in this post-Modern world—a world blown apart by knowledge and war, yet thrown together by technology and science. If we insist, as we usually do, that a liberal education emerges inevitably from taking a representative number of courses in all divisions of the curriculum, we may create only a mind torn against itself—unable to use what it knows because it sees only chaotic diversity, fragments of knowledge which paralyze rather than catalyze human resources. Education must indeed detach itself from the world's incessant demands, but it cannot deny them. If it would be relevant, education must recognize the existential and intellectual dilemmas of contemporary man, and it must find means of putting together meaningfully what the world appears to tear apart. Such a task may be common to most ages, but it is particularly acute in our era of radical transformation. For if opportunity creates only anomie to replace ideology, then the battle for an open society has been an ironic one indeed. Somehow we must discover channels to guide ourselves in a relativistic world. We must make limitless knowledge meaningful to the limited mind of the individual. In short, our question is: How may we integrate knowledge in a dis-integrated world?

TRADITION AND ANTI-INTELLECTUALISM

Some advocates of liberal education have opted to restore a "unified vision of man." We must, they insist, impose intellectual order upon our fragmenting world. We must re-charge our commitment to enduring values, and we must further resist the disintegrative and dehumanizing effects of science, technology and mass culture. Eliot's "heap of broken images" must be glued together with the cement of tradition and purpose.

Though it may appear satisfying emotionally and morally, this faith seems to be profoundly anti-intellectual; for it denies the testimony of today's most distinctive inquirers—that the world of contemporary man is no longer a metaphysical unity. The knot which once held our intellectual world together, which allotted to each particular discipline its unique purpose and function, has been hacked and slashed away. Because our contemporary world has become so rich and multi-dimensional, universalist ideologies have given way to a variety of differing disciplines and perspectives, no one or combination of which can claim to be comprehensive or even representative of the substantial world beyond our minds. We may retain our commitment to the quest for knowledge, but gone is the implicit faith that this knowledge will reveal a new secular cosmology to replace Christianity.

It is thus contemporary man's extraordinarily complex nature, not simply the modern division of labor, which has caused this fragmenting of unified visions. And it is our very knowledge which has revealed this complexity. To overcome fragmentation and dis-integration by forcing unity would thus be to deny what our own insights have taught us. In an age which pretends to social and institutional differentiation, which promotes equality of opportunity and freedom of thought and inquiry, such a unified vision of man is a chimera, a utopian or Edenic quest for certainty. It ignores cause (complexity and opportunity) by proposing to alleviate effect (intellectual fragmentation and moral anomie). Division of labor is an inevitable condition of contemporary civilization, one we cannot escape; we can only ask that in education it reflect actual issues in the lives of man, not arbitrary categories which further divide and alienate humans from existential realities.

Liberal education has heretofore been justly esteemed because it has done certain things, not simply because it has incorporated the liberal arts. In such an age as ours, we are forced back to first principles in asking what these things are. Before selecting the disciplines crucial to a liberating education, then, we had better define the goals.

EDUCATION FOR INDEPENDENCE

Education, as I interpret it, is fundamentally concerned with shaping critical and independent thinkers, students capable of getting along outside the formal institutional structure of courses and lectures and examinations. Thus, in the profoundest sense, under-graduate education is a preparation for post-undergraduate life—whether the student become college professor, business executive or Peace Corps worker.

Because it is necessarily preparation, and preparation in a world of fundamental intellectual revolutions, education should be essentially methodological rather than substantive. What matters is that the student know what to look for and where to look for it, not simply that he assimilate what inquirers before him have discovered.

Education must further hook into the student's value struc-ture, shaking the existential foundations of his thought and expe-rience. The Jacob report (10) in the mid-fifties has told us how ineffective formal education has been in tapping student values—even in the social sciences, where values readily emerge for challenge.

Finally, education should sensitize one to discovering the uni-versal in the particular, the particular in the universal. The student should be capable of, say, exploring the universe writ small in *Moby Dick,* and of subjecting the theory of class struggle to the most de-tailed particular criticism.

Traditionally the disciplines have provided the most effective institutional channel for imparting a liberal education. But are those disciplines now adequate to such a task? Do they reflect a division of labor relevant to issues in our post-Modern world, or do they impose historically-developed categories now inadequate to our deepest experiences? I suggest that the traditional disciplines are no longer fully adequate, and that supplementary categories must be devel-oped to revitalize the college curriculum. Let me attempt to substan-tiate this charge.

ARCHAIC DISCIPLINES

First, scholars have been unable to keep pace with the explod-ing body of knowledge in their own particular fields, let alone in related areas. Hosts of sub-fields have proliferated—urban sociology, diplomatic history, labor economics, comparative politics—and mastering even one of these sub-fields has become increasingly difficult.

As a result, there is almost as much diversity of orientation and individual temperament within the disciplines as between them. An economic theorist may have less in common with an economic statistician than with, say, a systematic social philosopher. That both the theorist and the statistician are labelled economists is secondary; the methodological difference between their approaches is more fundamental than the substantive unity of their disciplines.

This sort of labor division causes each discipline to reproduce within itself perspectives used in almost all other disciplines. In literature, for example, are to be found the perspectives of romantic aestheticians, pure artists, moralists, formalists, empiricists. And so also, with varying emphases, do perspectives proliferate in mathematics, in psychology, in philosophy, in physics, indeed even in history. To call a scholar a sociologist tells us less about him and his distinctive area of expertise than to call him, say, a rationalist or an empiricist.

It is almost meaningless, then, to suggest in curriculum planning that students must take courses in literature or in sociology or in history. The point is: What kind of literature? What kind of sociology? What kind of history? For each discipline is almost as diverse and fragmented as the world about us. Such diversity is not only inescapable but necessary to maintain intellectual richness and vitality within each field of inquiry. But this fact commands the recognition that coherence and structure in the college curriculum can no longer be found primarily in the disciplines themselves. Rather, they must be found in those orientations—functional, theoretical, empirical, moral, impressionistic—criss-crossing between the traditional fields.

More thorough study of the origins and history of disciplines would, I suspect, add substance to the charge (5, 8, 17, 21). That knowledge and its dissemination must be organized and systematized is obvious (3, 11, 19), but that the disciplines as traditionally constituted effectively discharge this function is questionable. We in the educational profession have yet to develop the institutional self-consciousness—the knowledge of traditions, their origins, growth, and rationale; the understanding of dominant mores and myths; the awareness of their historic relation to broad cultural and trans-cultural forces—which we urge upon those in society at large. Like other institutions, ours has developed pragmatically in a somewhat less than rational manner; and in some of the disciplines there is a pretense to status and narrowly-defined rigor which has cut off the richness and depth requisite to inquiring scholarship.

INHIBITING CATEGORIES

Like the modern ideologies which often reflect the provincial borders of our intellectual disciplines by reducing man to *only* his economic, or *only* his psychological, or *only* his technological or *only* his political dimension, these convenient categories have sometimes shielded us from the rich texture of existential reality. Particularly within the large university framework, disciplines have often served as channels for gaining status and identity and as convenient security niches from which to categorize scholars working in alien fields. Such categorization has in the academic world been perhaps as inhibiting internally as have external political pressures in prohibiting the release of free intellectual energies.

Finally, the creative leaders in many of the disciplines— Adolf Berle in economics, Henry Murray in psychology, Talcott Parsons in sociology, Paul Tillich in religion, Richard Hofstadter in history, F. O. Matthiessen in literature, Margaret Mead in anthropology—provide a most powerful critique of traditional departmentalism. For they have always felt impelled to expand beyond their respective specialties, both to satisfy their own intellectual curiosity and to add the substantive breadth which has made them leaders in their particular fields.

Even apart from the world beyond the university, then, the testimony of the disciplines themselves shatters their claim to being the sole institutions for organizing and imparting knowledge. A disciplinary education neither represents the world effectively nor the world of scholarship itself. But this criticism only defines the problem; to suggest a viable alternative is not so simple.

INTERDISCIPLINARY EFFORTS

As a means of avoiding premature specialization, one alternative has been simply to combine two or more disciplines and pursue interdisciplinary education. But this has its profound shortcomings, too. For often such an interdisciplinary orientation has been seized upon as a panacea by those lacking the patience or commitment or depth requisite to master difficult issues. The "problems" approach of progressive educators often drained intellectual content from knowledge as a means of superficially stimulating student enthusiasm. And even when this has not been true, the attempt to relate together entire fields does not help us integrate in a dis-integrated world. For if mastering one discipline is now impossible, how much more precarious it is to pretend knowledge of two or three. Such an interdisciplinary attitude is bound to meet the charge of dilettantism, a charge which in this context seems largely justified.

This, then, seems to be the situation of the modern scholar-teacher. He lives in a world where intellectual unity can no longer be assumed. He cannot trust that combining all the disciplines will add up to an integrative or liberating education, for the disciplines themselves reflect this dis-integrating world. He cannot hope to master even one of the fields, for our sum stock of information has been expanding at an exponential rate. If in such a world he strives for Renaissance universality, he may end with only a mass of diverse fragments. If he remains rooted to his own field, he refuses to consider issues in all their human complexity. And all this apart from his teaching responsibilities; for if he is to engage students critically in meaningful intellectual pursuits, he must somehow overcome these barriers by more than personal charisma.

He may despair at such a situation, but he need not. For the charge of dilettantism often levelled broadcast at all interdisciplinary efforts is legitimate only if the world is organized fundamentally according to the disciplines. If the world is not so organized, then it is the disciplinary specialist who may well be the dilettante; for he may remain satisfied with partial perspectives on, and premature solutions to, intellectual problems which transcend his particular horizons.

EXISTENTIAL GUIDELINES

It is a trite but too-often-ignored truth that vital knowledge must be about the world of man and nature, not the world of the university. We in academe have levelled incisive critiques at the blinders men use to shield themselves from the threatening insecurity of existential reality. But our own blinders remain ignored; and among the most powerful of intellectual barriers are the institutions, prejudices, and ideologies which define limits which the inquiring student may transcend only at his peril.

Why not, then, turn to the world of human experience for guidelines in organizing our curriculum in this emerging multiverse? Might we alert ourselves more directly to the worlds in which our students and our subjects live, and formulate an education which speaks clearly to and from those worlds? Such an education might be both integrative and vital, for it should be directly cognizant of those worlds' variety, richness and wholeness. If one begins there and temporarily by-passes the disciplines, he may then cut away the maze of petty burdens inhibiting his scholarly efforts.

Why, for example, should the French Revolution be delegated just to historians or *War and Peace* to literature courses? Essentially, one supposes, because the former is defined as an historical event and the latter as a novel; so academic categories have placed them in their appropriate boxes. But an attempt to understand either in full context would necessarily find the academic boxes too limiting. Why shouldn't the French Revolution be studied in sociology, say, as well as in history, or *War and Peace* in history as well as in literature? Certainly the former provides an abundant laboratory for sociological inquiry, and the latter a panorama of historical processes. If historians argue that sociologists understand too little about historical data and method, one may counter that historians have made few efforts systematically to comprehend the intricate relations between social structure, ideology, social change and personality formation (4, 7, 14, 16). If the sociological method "freezes" an historical era much as a still camera freezes a scene from nature, like the still picture it nonetheless affords a much better opportunity for detailed investigation of interrelationships than does the narrative "moving camera" picture of the historian. The Heisenberg principle has demonstrated that physical reality is complex enough to require understanding from more than one perspective; perhaps a re-thinking of social and literary categories may show that human reality is at least as complex.

Granted, a few adventurous scholars have already made the sort of leaps advocated here, but none may contend that our entire educational system has been pushed in this direction. And thus students are deprived of the intellectual adventures which make scholarly inquiry enriching to its most distinguished practitioners.

RISK AND REORIENTATION

The point is that our dis-integrated world allows, indeed demands, such attempts at reorientation. The unique fact of our post-Modern world is not simply anxiety but its correlate—opportunity. From our position of self-acknowledged intellectual insecurity, we may re-open the premature closures of more secure thought patterns in past ages. A dis-integrated world means that all stops are open, that anything may be tried, that the inquirer may if he wishes investigate possible relationships between toilet training and national character. He cannot in his integrative efforts refer to a metaphysical World View which assumes the world a unity with all its various parts cohering together, but he may explore a rich variety of hypothetical relationships between phenomena which at first glance seem to be separate (9, 20). The quest for integration thus becomes open and empirical, not deductive and metaphysical.

What is lost in security may be gained in variability and intellectual abundance.

Now we know, for example, that sufficient understanding of any historical period must include critical and systematic inquiry (13) into social structure, relationships between ideology and society, and between society and its imaginative productions in literature and the arts. Sometimes the initial hypothetical relationships prove upon inspection to be non-existent and rarely are they direct; but the adventure of searching is always meaningful and often rewarding in unexpected ways.

The ideal, then, should be the scholar who begins his study with a problem. He will attempt approaching the problem as a *tabula rasa*, then bring to bear upon it whatever techniques or information its distinctive texture suggests. In one situation he may detect psychological determination, in another technological, in yet another a multiplicity of causes no one of which emerges as primary. He will not ignore the disciplines, but will draw freely upon them only after he attempts directly approaching his problem and allows it to define its own relevant questions.

His subject for integrative study may be broader than that of the traditional disciplinary scholar, but it need not be. His first concern, however, is to view the particular details of his problem in the light of its potential broader consequences. He continually wants to know the significance of things. There will of course be human limits to what he can do or learn, but he will define these for himself rather than let his discipline do it for him. He thus will attempt to counteract not specialization per se, for he too seeks depth, but rather a specialization unaware of the general significance of its limited topic.

EXEMPLAR OF INTEGRATION

Lest an ideal and unrealizable abstraction be created here, let me illustrate by presenting a specific case of admirable and effective integration. I refer to Erik Erikson's *Young Man Luther* (6).

A psychoanalytically trained psychiatrist, Erikson has devoted much of his time and energy to working with emotionally disturbed youth. A cursory reaction, then, shows him clearly beyond his field of expertise in pretending to deepen our understanding of a figure in history. Yet as one proceeds through *Young Man Luther,* it becomes increasingly clear that Erikson's psychoanalytic training has uniquely qualified him for this historical task; and because of it he has moved beyond trained specialists whose breadth of knowledge in history as such may be far greater.

For Erikson's focus is limited, so limited that he had originally planned the study of Luther to comprise only a single chapter in a book on emotional crises in late adolescence and early adulthood. But as he inquired further into the central purpose of the study— to reveal young Martin Luther's crisis of identity—Erikson's integrative mind continually expanded beyond the usual limits set to historical studies.

Throughout the book his focus is never diffuse; yet to reveal in full context Luther's identity crisis, Erikson finds it necessary to study, analyze and explain aspects of the following: the structure of ideology and its relation to the quest for identity; the sociology of the medieval peasant; politics and economics in the Holy Roman Empire; the social psychology of the Luther family; the conversion of St. Paul and of a Yurok Indian woman as compared and contrasted with that of Luther; the history of the Augustinian monk-early adulthood; anxiety in Adolf Hitler as compared and contrasted with that of Luther; the history of the Augustinian monkhood; the psychological meaning of the mass; the meaning of the psychoanalyst's own early analysis; the history of early Christianity, its initial purism and later consequent bureaucracy; the importance of technology and particularly the printing press in providing historically-vital channels for Luther's religious rebellion; the advent of rising nationalism in the 15th and 16th centuries; a close textual analysis of Luther's writings (an analysis, incidentally, which in rhetorical sensitivity would do justice to the techniques of the New Criticism in poetry); a description of relationships between human physiology and ideology; and finally a vivid parallel between the

Reformation of the 16th century and contemporary tendencies in a little fishing village by Lake Chapala in Mexico, where Erikson finished writing his book.

AUTONOMOUS DIMENSIONS

Disciplinary scholars might object to Erikson's interpretation. The economist might find too little economics, the theologian too little theology, the sociologist too little sociology, the historian too little history. But no one should object that it has too little Martin Luther. And that, after all, is the point. For Erikson, Luther was an individual influenced by and influencing a host of varying forces. In order as a psychiatrist to understand Luther's compulsive quest for identity, he must investigate how general cultural configurations were specifically refracted in the personality of this particular historical figure. Some forces were essentially psychological, others appeared fundamentally religious, yet others economic or political or sociological. Erikson never attempts to reduce them to a single primary focus. Rather, he respects the autonomy of each dimension —historical, philosophical, sociological, cultural, economic, geographical, religious—tracing the influence of each as far as he responsibly can in understanding Luther, and no further. He is fundamentally concerned with seeing them all through the filter of Luther's identity crisis, but he does not reduce them to that crisis. Each dimension of the culture and each comparison with trans-cultural perspectives is analyzed generally on its own terms, then particularly as it affected Luther.

Erikson has thus accomplished a piece of brilliant and humane scholarship because his focus is narrow but deep; and because of its depth it is wide-ranging in consequence. He has concentrated on a problem—revealing Luther's identity crisis—and has felt impelled to draw from the disciplines in whatever manner his problem demands it. The resulting book is a liberating education in itself, a model of integrative scholarship in a dis-integrated and therefore open-ended world.

One cannot insist that all students and teachers attain the insight and vision of an Erik Erikson. But teachers can provide opportunities for this type of orientation to flower. Instead of allowing only the Eriksons to attempt projects like this, they might be encouraging students at even the introductory undergraduate stages to such creative inquiry. Ordinarily, they tolerate such integrative efforts only from bright students who have already shown competence in particular disciplines. But what is there about the structure of a discipline—as opposed to an integrative orientation—which makes it a prerequisite for attacking vital issues? Why not meaningfully engage students in such rich existential problems at the beginning of their educational experience?

PROPOSED PERSPECTIVES

Why not, for example, introduce students to social science perspectives through such courses as "Approaches to the Self and Reality" (Sarah Lawrence); "Freedom, Authority and Decision-Making" (Shimer); "Conflict, Equilibrium and Consensus" (Shimer)? Or to humanistic perspectives through "Mimesis" (Monteith); "Myth, Ritual and Literature" (Bennington); "Poetry and the Imaginative Process" (Bennington); "Art as Propaganda in the Modern World" (Monteith)? Or to natural science perspectives through "The Evolutionary Hypothesis" (Monteith); "Biology, Human Physiology and Behavior" (Sarah Lawrence); "Atomism" (Monteith)? Here, it seems, are courses meaningfully integrating material designed to tap vital interests and abilities of students, courses reflecting and critically analyzing this dis-integrated multiverse which we now experience.

Meaningful integration may come from several differing perspectives—from a depth concentration on themes, on relatively limited geographical or cultural areas, on methods of inquiry, on political or social problems, on particular individuals or cultural movements, on institutions or processes, on relatively brief historical periods, and so on. This is of course sometimes practiced at advanced levels, but only after the student is so attuned to his own discipline that he may have phased out alternative perspectives.

We should, then, become flexible enough to experiment beyond (1) the "building-block" theory of education which requires students to master discipline-oriented texts and introductory surveys prior to allowing them to hook deeply into actual existential situations, and (2) a Lockean faculty psychology which (a) assumes the student a blank tablet which must be exposed to all the various disciplines and thus "learn" their consequent "skills" and (b) envisions the professor as simply the exemplar of his own unidimensional discipline.

When we allow students to tackle such issues early in their intellectual development, we may find them becoming intensely concerned over their courses and capable occasionally of producing remarkable pieces of profound and creative scholarship. They should become engaged because life and learning will be shown to have a common intellectual texture and existential drama. And they may become more profound intellectually by appreciating the depth, richness and variety of perspectives available to approach particular problems. If students probe deeply into only a few problems, be they historical or literary or sociological, then they should become acutely aware of how superficial their knowledge is in areas they have not probed into. But if they are forced to skate lightly over the surface of an ice-like mass of discipline-oriented information, they may never learn what comprehensive depth is. Thus integration of this type should foster both depth and respect for breadth, a concentrated focus and an appreciation for alternative foci. If we can implement such integrative education meaningfully, we may break the vicious cycle of dull and superficial courses producing dull and superficial students who in turn bore their dismayed professors.[1]

---

[1] I wish to acknowledge that my experience at Raymond College, the University of the Pacific's experimental honors college in liberal education, has profoundly affected my thinking on this subject and continually renewed my

INTEGRATIVE ALTERNATIVES

To sum up: When planning curriculum, we have been dominated by the unacknowledged assumption that disciplines are things, real entities which both order and structure our knowledge and adequately reflect processes of life beyond the world of academe. I suggest instead that disciplines are rather kaleidoscope patch-works of institutions and mores, having developed in response to a host of particular problems but not reflecting any over-all rational plan. If these disciplines ever did have substantial relation to the acting world of men, ideas and things, such a relation is dis-integrating in our post-Modern world of radically new experiences amidst new values.

Obviously, I have capitalized upon the intellectual's option to simplify issues in order to present them in clear outline. Disciplines do have a rationale—if not a metaphysical one written into the structure of reality, then certainly a pragmatic one responding to the need for order and systematic knowledge. Further, problems are not simply "given"; our response to them depends upon the orientation we bring to their study, and that orientation will be affected by pre-existing disciplinary concepts. But the issue here is not whether disciplines must be replaced, but whether they should be supplemented. Disciplines, I submit, have been reified and institutionalized to such a degree that in curriculum planning we have difficulty thinking beyond them. In such a situation and in such a world, a plea for alternative categories seems imperative.

Also, I have of necessity resorted to the standard practice of the idealist critic—contrasting institutionalized realities with conceptualized ideals. Were the ideals urged here to be implemented, they too might soon routinize, and thus become subject to many

faith that an education which taps deeply into student values can produce significant results. I wish also to thank Provost Warren Bryan Martin for offering useful criticism of a draft of this essay and Dr. Jerry Gaff for the original conversation which provided the genesis for the piece.

of the same critiques here levelled at disciplinary education. But the spectre of potential bureaucracy should not bind us to the tepid tentacles of the status quo.

It is true that we shall not work magic tomorrow simply by altering the structure of our curriculum. Institutional inertia, the perhaps necessary use of disciplines as the primary mechanisms for organizing and systematizing knowledge, the necessity for maintaining some stable structure in the education of the student, the present training of college teachers in disciplinary-ruled graduate schools and the demands of graduate departments for earlier undergraduate field specialization—all these militate against too drastic a change in the present system. Yet if ours among all professions and institutions professes the free and creative inquiry into truth and the vital and impartial communication of those truths we discover, then it behooves us at least to experiment with new means of implementing liberal, integrative education. In a dis-integrating multiverse of anxiety and opportunity, we can responsibly do no less.

REFERENCES

1. BELL, D. *The end of ideology: On the exhaustion of political ideas in the fifties.* NY: Collier Books, 1961.

2. BELL, D. (Ed.) *The radical right.* Garden City, NY: Doubleday Anchor, 1964.

3. BRUNER, J. *The process of education.* Cambridge: Harvard Univ. Pr., 1960.

4. CAHNMAN, W., and BOSKOFF, A. (Eds.) *Sociology and history: Theory and research.* NY: Free Press, 1964.

5. DUVERGER, M. *An introduction to the social sciences.* NY: Praeger, 1964.

6. ERIKSON, E. *Young man Luther: A study in psychoanalysis and history.* NY: W. W. Norton, 1962.

7. HOFSTADTER, R. History and the social sciences. In Stern, F. (Ed.) *The varieties of history.* NY: Meridian, 1956. Pp. 359–370.

8. HOSELITZ, B. The social sciences in the last two hundred years. In

Hoselitz (Ed.) *A reader's guide to the social sciences.* Glencoe, Ill.: Free Press, 1959. Pp. 7–25.

9. HUGHES, H. S. *Consciousness and society: The reorientation of European social thought, 1890–1930.* NY: Vintage Books, n.d.

10. JACOB, P. *Changing values in college.* NY: Harper, 1957.

11. KLIEBARD, H. M. Structure of the disciplines as an educational slogan, *Teach. Coll. Rec.,* 1965, *66,* 598–603.

12. LIPSET, S. M. *Political man: The social bases of politics.* Garden City, NY: Doubleday Anchor, 1963.

13. See, as examples of area studies breaking through traditional categories: Marx, L. *The machine in the garden: Technology and the pastoral ideal in America,* NY: Oxford Univ. Pr., 1964, and Smith, H. N. *Virgin land: The American west as symbol and myth,* NY: Vintage Books, [1957; Cambridge: Harvard University Press, 1950].

14. MAZLISH, B. (Ed.) *Psychoanalysis and history.* Englewood Cliffs, NJ: Prentice-Hall, 1963.

15. PHENIX, P. H. The disciplines as curriculum content. In Passow, H. W. (Ed.) *Curriculum crossroads,* NY: Teach. Coll. Pr., 1962.

16. POTTER, D. *People of plenty: Economic abundance and the American character.* Chicago: Univ. of Chicago Pr., 1960.

17. SALOMON, E. *The tyranny of progress.* NY: Noonday Pr., 1955.

18. SAVETH, E. (Ed.) *American history and the social sciences.* NY: Free Press, 1964.

19. SCHWAB, J. J. The concept of the structure of a discipline, *Educ. Rec.,* 1962, *43,* pp. 107–125.

20. WEBER, M. *The methodology of the social sciences.* Glencoe, Ill.: Free Press, 1949.

21. ZNANIECKI, F. *Cultural sciences: Their origins and development.* Urbana, Ill.: Univ. of Illinois Pr., 1952.

RELEVANCE
AND THE CURRICULUM

LAWRENCE E. METCALF AND MAURICE P. HUNT

Without any doubt the rallying cry of most people calling for curriculum reform has been "relevancy." The curriculum, they say, needs to be relevant if it is to appeal to today's student because the existing curriculum is out of date. Indeed, ever since the days when Harold Benjamin published **The Saber-Tooth Curriculum** in 1939 demonstrating the salient weaknesses of the obsolete curriculum of paleolithic man, the call for relevancy has always been loud. However, many critics have significantly forgotten to specify what would constitute a relevant curriculum. Not so Metcalf and Hunt.

Metcalf and Hunt boldly call for a relevant curriculum and go on to explicate their position. For them a relevant curriculum is one that deals with an important social movement in today's world, namely, the rejection of adult culture by youth. They specify four assumptions, issues, or propositions involved in this youth movement and state that a relevant curriculum would "make their study [a study of these four assumptions] a major purpose of general education." Thus, the authors' relevant curriculum, which stems from a social issue rather than the disciplines or from everyday life activities, is not a mere insignificant part of the school program.

The connections between this proposal by Metcalf and Hunt and those by Hand (Chapter 4), Mann (Chapter 9), and Wise (Chapter 7) go beyond first appearances. Also, the rationale for having the student investigate "problems of the larger culture" rather than "personal problems" deserves careful consideration and discussion among curriculum workers. Are Metcalf and Hunt correct in stating that their approach is more promising than programs, such as black studies, which also claim to be relevant?

◇◇◇◇◇◇◇◇◇◇◇◇◇◇◇◇◇◇◇◇◇◇◇◇◇◇◇◇◇◇◇◇◇◇◇◇◇◇◇

Our assignment in this article is to indicate what we mean by a relevant curriculum. We shall define curriculum not as "all the experiences a child or youth has in school" but more traditionally as "the formal course-work taken by students." We believe that formal coursework acquires relevance whenever it impinges upon what students believe, and whenever it has the effect of producing a pattern of belief that is well-grounded and internally consistent.

Ours is a period of history in which youth on a mass and international scale reject the culture of the old. This rejection is not universal to all youth; some are more actively opposed to established traditions; many are in tacit support of changes initiated by the bolder and more aggressive young. To a large extent the rebellion of the young began with college students, has now been adopted by large numbers of high school students, and is beginning to filter down into junior high school. Young people are beginning to develop their own culture, and appear at times to learn more from one

"Relevance and the Curriculum" by Lawrence E. Metcalf and Maurice P. Hunt is reprinted with permission from *Phi Delta Kappan,* 51 (March, 1970): 358–61.

another than from teachers or parents. Some adults feel so turned off and rejected that they doubt that they can ever say anything that youth would accept as relevant.

Youth's rejection of adult culture—"the whole, rotten, stinking mess of it"—has become a significant social movement. This movement has assumed international proportions—practically every modern, industrialized nation has felt its impact. Any school that has not made this social movement a subject of serious study on the part of its youthful clientele is about as irrelevant as it can get.

Rejection of adult culture is proclaimed overtly, not merely by verbal attack, but also by deliberate adoption of grooming habits or display of those artifacts which have been established or promoted as symbols of sophisticated rebellion. New hair styles, manners of dress, a new language (which relies heavily on traditional Anglo-Saxon monosyllables), a new music, an open sexual promiscuity, and the use of drugs or pot—all reflect a wholesale rejection of tradition and orthodoxy.

Many of the new values and customs are carefully chosen as goads to older persons. "What would my parents or grandparents least like to have me think and see me do?" When this question has been answered, often only after some tests of adult reaction, the young then adopt whatever they think will best demonstrate that they are *not* part of the main culture stream of earlier generations. In the case of males, it may require only long hair and a string of beads to make the point. For females, attendance at a love-in or rock festival attired in a mini-miniskirt may suffice. The movement has its uniforms, rituals, and badges of membership. Older people sometimes put on the uniform in order to demonstrate that they are not entirely out of sympathy with the ideas and ideals of youth. Others, who are not without sympathy, refuse the beard and the beads simply because they detest all uniforms, whether worn by pigs, fascists, or revolutionaries.

But the rebelliousness of youth does not confine itself to the symbolisms of dress, language, and coiffure. Rejection of religion as traditionally practiced has become commonplace. New faiths are emergent, as among the hippies, and have more in common with

Zen than anything orthodox to Christianity. Paul Goodman sees the young as primarily religious. If so, theirs is the kind of faith that mirrors John Dewey's distinction between religion and the religious.*

Equally significant is the anti-war and pro-love stance of our young rebels. When generalized to embrace a way of life, it runs contrary to most American traditions. We now see mass protests on a grand scale. Riots, marches, sit-ins, love-ins, and mass assemblies surpass anything in our history. When a war moratorium brings hundreds of thousands of persons into public arenas, it can truly be called a "happening." Adults are puzzled by it all, and somewhat frightened.

A CONCEPT OF RELEVANT CURRICULUM

Young people are particularly critical of established educational practice. A common charge is that education lacks relevance. Often this criticism harks back to some of the traditions of old progressives in education. Sometimes, the charge means that education has not allied itself with the goals of revolutionaries, or that it has allied itself with business, labor, and the military.

What can education do these days that would be relevant? *We suggest that the schools incorporate in their curriculum a study of an important social movement, rejection by youth, and that this study emphasize examining, testing, and appraising the major beliefs caught up in this movement.* To pander to the instincts or impulses of rebellion would have little or no educational effect. The over-30 adult who simply "eggs on" his activist students does his clientele no service. A black studies program that fosters black nationalism or separatism would be equally obnoxious. If this is what youths mean by relevance, their wishes can not be served.

Students find it all too easy to spot contradictions in the beliefs of their elders, and to explain all such discrepancies as instances of

---

* See John Dewey, *A Common Faith.*

hypocrisy. They are a good deal less proficient in spotting their own inconsistencies, and they are quite convinced of their own sincerity. We need the kind of educational relevance that would help and require young people to examine their most basic assumptions about the kind of world that exists, and how they propose to change the world from what it is into something preferable. Students who rebel not only against the establishment but also against logical analysis may not at first perceive the relevance of this kind of education.

In order to achieve this kind of relevance, teachers will have to familiarize themselves with the thought patterns of students— their attitudes, values, beliefs, and interests. This can be done. It helps just to listen carefully to what young people are saying. Sometimes teachers who listen do not bore deeply enough into the meaning of what has been heard. They learn much about the surface thought of students but little, if anything, about what students "really think."

If we look closely at what students today believe, four issues or propositions in social analysis and processes of social change seem to prevail within the movement. Taken together, these four issues suggest a rejection of the liberal-reformist tradition. Liberalism is anathema to our youthful rebels. Liberalism is a failure, they say. Liberals talk much and do little. Many of the young leaders resemble the romantics who supported totalitarian movements in pre-war Germany and Italy. A seldom observed and reported fact is that the candidacy of George Wallace in 1968 received more support from people under than over 30 years of age. A realignment in American politics that would place radicals and conservatives in alliance against liberalism is not without prospect.

A major issue that divides radicals from liberals is to be found in attitudes toward The System. Liberals tend to assume that the system can best be changed and improved by working within it. They may agree with radicals that much in the system requires fundamental and sweeping change, but they also believe that the system is basically sound in that it permits and values change when rationally determined and implemented. In contrast, the radical would work against the system from the outside. He wants no part of the system, which he views as rotten throughout.

Liberals who suggest that schools assist students to examine the system in order to determine whether it is as rotten as some claim it to be are regarded as advocates of a delaying action. Radicals tend to view analysis of this kind as a form of social paralysis. It is not clearly established how many of today's young can properly be classified as radicals. An increasing number do believe that social change must begin with a total rejection of the existing system. Drastic change is preferred to any attempt to patch the existing system.

A second assumption that divides young people from the mainstream of American liberalism is over the relationship of means to ends. Liberals tend toward the assumption that the achievement of democratic ends requires the use of democratic means. Every means is an end, and every end a means to some further end. The quality of any end we achieve cannot be separated from the quality of the means used to achieve it. In contrast, many of the young assume that our kind of society can be transformed into a more democratic system only as people dare to employ undemocratic methods. They see no inconsistency in advocacy of free speech and denial of such freedom to their opposition. Some liberals agree with radicals on the need for drastic changes in the system, but they are unwilling to achieve such change except through processes of reason and persuasion.

A third assumption expresses on the part of the young a preference for intuitive and involved thinking as opposed to rational and detached thought. Many of the hippies, for example, have voiced a distaste for the logic and rationality of middle-class Americans. In contrast, liberals have criticized middle-class Americans for not being rational enough.

A part of the issue here is over the nature of rationality. Liberals do not agree that rational thought is necessarily detached or without involvement. Thought springs from the ground of social perplexity and concern. Objectivity is not the same as neutrality. Objectivity is a means by which to express concern and achieve conclusions. It is not to be used as a method by which to avoid conclusions or commitments. In the hands of some liberals, however, it has appeared to be a method by which to avoid rather than make value judgments. When they perceive objectivity as avoidance, concerned youth will look elsewhere for their philosophy. An intuition or existential leap may be their solution to any confusion that inhabits their minds. The popularity of the drug experience as a source of awareness and insight is consistent with this preference for intuitive methods of problem solving. The growing interest in parapsychology, extrasensory perception, spiritualism, and various versions of the occult manifests the same tendency to retreat from the use of reason in the study of social affairs.

A fourth assumption, issue, or proposition is over the nature, worth, and necessity of violence. The liberal eschews violence except when an organized minority thwarts the will of the majority, if that will seems to be the outcome of free discussion and reflective study of alternatives. The young, on the other hand, often regard reason and discussion as forms of compromise. It is quite defensible to take the law into one's hands if the law is unjust. One does not obey an unjust law until one is able to persuade others of its injustice and thus get it changed. Evasion of the law or open refusal to obey the law is an acceptable form of social protest, if personal conscience so dictates.

Basic to this issue is the question of whether or not drastic system change can be achieved without use of violence. Advocates of violence have not always distinguished between impressionistic and instrumental violence.* Impressionistic violence is the kind of hot response that results from deep-seated frustration over existing social conditions. Instrumental violence is more disciplined in nature, and is followed deliberately and coolly as a method of social protest with social change as its objective.

---

* Charles Hamilton is to be credited with this distinction, as developed in a speech at Wingspread in 1968.

The above four assumptions are basic in varying degree to the life outlook of young people who are in rebellion against established traditions. None of them is entirely new. Each has been tried and tested in a variety of social circumstances. Relevant history would reveal where such assumptions lead when acted upon under certain conditions. Yet none of these assumptions is today subjected to open, careful, and fair appraisal by a majority of schools or teachers. A relevant curriculum would take these assumptions seriously enough to make their study a major purpose of general education. Such study would help young people to understand their important personal problems but would also open up for serious study the large social problems of our time.

UTOPIAS, RELEVANT AND IRRELEVANT *

A curriculum that would assist young people in an examination of their basic assumptions about society and its improvement must deal with values and social policies. Yet attention to values and social policies is now almost totally foreign to public schools.

Young people today will be in the prime of life by the year 2000. They can begin to think now about what they want as a society by that time. Four questions are basic to a curriculum that would start now to build toward future-planning: 1) What kind of society now exists, and what are the dominant trends within it? 2) What kind of society is likely to emerge in the near future, let us say by the year 2000, if present trends continue? 3) What kind of society is preferable, given one's values? 4) If the likely and prognosticated society is different from the society that one prefers, what can the individual, alone or as a member of groups, do toward eliminating the discrepancy between prognostication and preference, between expectation and desire?

---

* We are indebted to Saul Mendlovitz of the World Law Fund, who is also professor of international law, Rutgers University, for development of the concept of relevant utopias.

These questions are relevant to anyone, but they are particularly relevant to those young people who think in utopias and who agree with Buckminster Fuller that we now have to choose between utopia and oblivion.

We define utopia as any description of a society radically different from the existing one. Some utopias, as described, are relevant. Others are irrelevant. A relevant utopia is a model of a reformed world which not only spells out in specific and precise behavioral detail the contents of that new world but, in addition, provides a behavioral description of the transition to be made from the present system to the utopian one. Irrelevant utopias omit all solutions to the problem of transition. They may be precisely defined in behavioral terms, as in Butler's Erewhon, but provide no suggestions as to how one gets from where he is to where he wants to be.

Most utopias stated or implied by today's youth are irrelevant. Youth are fairly clear as to what they oppose. They desire a drastically different kind of social system, but they are not clear in any detailed sense as to what they desire as a system, or how that undefined system might be brought into being. To be relevant, youth with encouragement from the schools will have to engage in the kind of hard thinking that results in construction of social models. Hard thinking and model building are not always prized by youth who rely upon intuition and hunches for solutions to problems. Intuition is good enough for stating irrevelant utopias. It will not work, however, for those who value precisely stated concepts and tested solutions to the problem of social transition.

The search for relevant utopias should have great appeal to those youth who feel or believe that a drastic change in the social system is required for solution of today's problems. Its appeal lies in the fact that the search for relevance requires one to take seriously, and not merely romantically, the problem of how best to achieve drastic system change. Since drastic system change has occurred in the past, some study of a certain kind of history—not the kind usually taught in the schools—should be relevant to this search.

RELEVANT UTOPIAS, PREFERRED WORLDS

We have defined as a relevant utopia any social vision or dream that has been expressed as a social model with due regard for problems of precise definition and successful transition. From studies of existing society numerous relevant utopias have been stated. In the area of international systems alone no less than nine models have been identified by Falk and Mendlovitz.* Each model may be used descriptively, predictively, and prescriptively. That is, each may be seen as a report of what already exists, as a prediction of what will soon exist, or as a prescription of what ought to exist in the near future. (Obviously, a model used only for descriptive purposes does not function as any kind of utopia, relevant or irrelevant. A person who sees the present international system in certain terms can encounter in another person a different description. Both persons may agree or disagree as to what they conceive utopia to be.) Much of the literature fails to make a clear distinction between descriptive and other uses of a model. The methodology of relevant utopias requires that such distinctions be consciously made. This methodology also requires us to take seriously any utopia that qualifies as relevant. But to take it seriously does not force us to prefer it.

One chooses his preferred world from the set of relevant utopias available to him. It is in the region of preferred worlds that individuality as prized by young radicals has a chance to express itself. A person who chooses his preferred world from a set of available relevant utopias must decide what risks he is prepared to take; and obviously, persons differ greatly as to what risks they perceive and what risks they are willing to take.

An illustration from international relations and systems may serve to clarify this point. Grenville Clark and Louis Sohn have developed a relevant utopia that takes the form of limited world gov-

---

* Richard Falk and Saul Mendlovitz (eds.), *A Strategy of World Order.* New York: World Law Fund, 1966.

ernment. Their model consists of detailed amendments to the UN Charter which would give to the United Nations sufficient authority to prevent war, but without authority to intervene in the domestic affairs of nation states. Another model, developed by Robert Hutchins and his colleagues at the University of Chicago, envisages a much more sweeping kind of world authority. The relationship within their model between the world authority and the nation states resembles that which holds within the American federal system between the national government and the several states.

If one's choice is limited to these two models, which one should become one's preferred world? One can imagine a person who would say to himself: "The federal model is superior to the modified UN model for purposes of war prevention because it can get at the causes of war by intervening in the domestic affairs of nation states. But the likelihood that any such world authority will come into being by the year 2000 is very dim. Yet some kind of world government is necessary if we are to have any chance of avoiding large-scale nuclear war. Therefore, I choose Clark-Sohn as my preferred world." Someone else might argue as follows: "Without an effective world government, nuclear disaster is bound to occur. Clark-Sohn, although feasible by the year 2000, could not possibly work. Hutchins, though very difficult to achieve, is my preferred world. To work for anything less would be a waste of time. I'll risk everything on reaching for the impossible. Perhaps, my preference can even have some influence on the possibilities in the case."

Students have every right to differ with one another and with their teachers in their preferred worlds. They may also disagree as to whether a given utopia has been stated relevantly, as we have defined relevance. They may even disagree as to whether a particular utopia would be either effective, if adopted, or achievable if pursued with zeal and rationality. They may also disagree as to whether utopian solutions are as necessary as some social critics claim. But these various differences are not always qualitatively the same. Whether a given model would work, or whether a given model is achievable in the near future, are factual questions; such questions can be answered only by ascertaining as rationally as possible what the probable facts are. But a difference in opinion over preferred worlds is not always a factual difference. It may be a difference involving values, preferred risks, life styles, and even personal temperament. One may use logic and evidence in choosing his preferred world, but logical men in possession of all the facts may not always agree on the world they prefer.

PERSONAL DILEMMAS, SOCIAL CONCERNS

A relevant curriculum is sometimes defined as one addressed to the personal problems of youth. This is not good enough. *It is more relevant to engage young people in a study of the problems of the larger culture in which many of their personal problems have their origin. The culture of most significance to the young consists of those aspects that are problematic—that is, the large conflicts and confusions which translate into the conflicts and confusions of individuals.*

To take one example, young people who are opposed to the war in Vietnam are reluctant to take a position against all war because the larger culture from which most of their learning continues to come expresses the same reluctance. In fact, many of the young insist upon the right to be conscientiously opposed to the war in Vietnam without a requirement that out of conscience they oppose all war. When asked the four questions basic to the methodology of relevant utopias as applied to the Vietnamese (what is Vietnam like today, what will it be like in the near future if present trends are extrapolated, what would you like it to be, and what can you do about any discrepancy between extrapolation and values?), they are prone to reply that the fate of the Vietnamese is of no concern to them and that America should mind its own business. Their vaunted idealism is thus victimized by the widespread cultural preference for some form of isolationism. Although they don't like Nixon, they find it difficult to oppose his attempts to turn over the war to the Vietnamese. The methodology of relevant utopias would ask them to consider carefully whether or not Nixon's policies and their own view of those policies are at all adequate as steps transitional to a drastic change in the existing system of international relations. Unless they make an assessment of this kind, their opinions on a number of related personal and social matters are bound to reflect a great deal of confusion. They could end up as confused as the parents and grandparents whose views they reject.

Finally, what has been said about the use of relevant utopias in social analysis and prescription also applies to personal development and self-analysis. The significant questions are: What kind of person am I now? What kind will I become if present habits and trends persist? What kind of person would I like to become? What can be done now about tendencies and preferences that conflict? This approach to the problem of identity is more promising than some of the programs offered these days in the name of black studies, black history, and black pride. Historical and cultural studies have maximal relevance when they help us to predict the future or to make transition.

9

HIGH SCHOOL
STUDENT PROTEST AND
THE NEW CURRICULUM WORKER:
A Radical Alliance

JOHN S. MANN

That such a curriculum proposal focusing on student protest appeared by the early 1970's should be no surprise. The student protests
which began a decade earlier in the undergraduate colleges rapidly
spread to the high schools and even to some junior high schools and
elementary schools. When university students involved in the protest
movement entered into teaching, they soon began to see the possibility of creating a pre-college curriculum based on the very concerns
of the movement.

John Mann sees high school protest as a phenomenon that will
continue for some time because students feel exploited by the conditions of the currently established curriculum pattern. The rage students
feel is real, he claims, because the purposes of the schools are extrinsic

153

to their needs and the school environment is not humanistic nor can it be until a fundamental change occurs. Hence, Mann proposes a change in the curriculum rationale of Ralph Tyler (see the Introduction to this book) and a new focus as a "curricular response" to students.

Since Mann's proposal constitutes "an application of Deweyan theory," the reader should study its four dimensions in relation to the views of Dewey (Chapter 1). The connection between Mann's proposal and that of Metcalf and Hunt (Chapter 8) deserves close attention, especially the point concerning protest and rejection of adult culture. The reader should also refer to Kilpatrick (Chapter 2) and Wise (Chapter 7). Mann himself poses many questions in his article which the reader would do well to respond to as he reads this most recent curriculum proposal. But the reader must also respond to the question, "Is Mann's curriculum proposal for students and curriculum workers acceptable?"

<hr>

Today many groups of high school students are in process of identifying themselves as politically significant collectivities. By this I mean that students have begun to come together as groups under nobody's auspices but their own in order to affect policies that govern their lives. Since students are required by law to attend school, and since few other institutional associations are open to them, the policies of the school system to which they belong are of chief concern to them. Thus students have begun to demand increasing control over their educational fate.

A common response to this situation is to view it as a threat, as a discipline problem, as misbehavior. I would like to offer a differing view, one which discovers rich educational potential in student pro-

"High School Student Protest and the New Curriculum Worker: A Radical Alliance" by John S. Mann is reprinted with permission from *A New Look at Progressive Education*, 1972 Yearbook, James R. Squire, ed., (Washington, D.C.: Association for Supervision and Curriculum Development, 1972), pp. 325–44. Reprinted with permission of the Association for Supervision and Curriculum Development and John S. Mann. Copyright © 1972 by the Association for Supervision and Curriculum Development.

test, and, by so doing, also discovers a new political and educational role for educators whose commitments have their roots in the progressive conception of education.

The general plan for developing this view is as follows: First, I will make some general observations about the historic-intellectual situation of the public practitioner of education, and then I will make some general observations about the central thrust of high school student protest. These observations will converge upon the points of common intent between the student and the educator.

Next I will try to illuminate the "educational potential" I referred to. Then I will outline what I would regard as an appropriate curricular response to this potential.

THE PRACTITIONER IN PERSPECTIVE

The view is often expressed that the progressive education movement failed. The statement needs qualification, but certainly it is a part of the truth. The reasons given are many. One of the less well understood reasons has to do with the enormous intrinsic difficulty of the practical problems posed by Deweyan pedagogical theory. Central among these problems was that of giving rigorous operational meaning to such concepts as "interest" and "educative experience" and "end-in-view" and "choice." And why was this such a difficult problem? In part, at least, because "choice" and "pursuit of interest" and "end-in-view" are vacuous concepts outside of the context of the actual taking of responsibility for one's self and for others. And the authentic taking of responsibility on the part of the student was a condition progressively inclined schools found it difficult or impossible to synthesize in any real sense.

In the late thirties leading educators seemed to be making some progress with these difficult problems. Yet when the Progressive Education Association fell apart, the political thrust required to move school bureaucracies ahead with more refined efforts to build sound practice upon a Deweyan conceptual base dissolved. Subsequent events on a national political scale have brought other educative tendencies into monolithic prominence, and many educators of progressive inclination have had to be content with innocuous and futile rhetoric centering upon the *reactive* concept of "humanizing education." Why *"had* to be content . . ." and why is "humanizing education" a "reactive concept"? Let me explain with a digression which will make some important points en route.

Ralph Tyler's well-known monograph on curriculum and instruction may be taken as a concise expression of a dominant point of view about fundamental things. This point of view has come to be known as the "Tyler rationale" (1949).

The Tyler rationale has three parts to it: you decide what you want to accomplish, then you choose a way of accomplishing it, then you test whether you have actually accomplished it. The first part is crucial. How do you decide? Tyler tells us that first is the matter of value judgment. Then he tells us that this value judgment is taken care of by having the school staff agree upon a comprehensive philosophy of education. What follows is logical and simple, but it is insufficient because, upon examination, the proposition "getting a school staff to agree upon a philosophy of education" turns out to be exceedingly problematic. Achieving "agreement upon a philosophy of education" in the context of a democratic society is either impossible or meaningless. In the Tyler outlook, such agreement is equivalent to agreement upon those basic value propositions that provide the ultimate criteria for selecting the objectives for which a school is to work. Some familiarity with both the history of philosophical thought about education and the history of actual schooling makes it amply clear that such value propositions have as antecedents either beliefs about the nature of the Good or beliefs about the nature of society, or both.

Democracy is a way of arriving at workable compromise with a minimum of bloodshed, not a system for arriving at agreement on Truth (Wolff, Moore, and Marcuse, 1965). A school staff is responsible to a public which is heterogeneous in fundamental beliefs. It can agree to a compromise upon philosophy, but it is absurd to suppose that it can agree upon "a philosophy."

What is important about the difference? When you "agree upon a philosophy," everyone who is partner to the agreement believes the "philosophy" to be true. When you agree to compromise upon a "philosophy," *no one* believes the compromise to be true.

By and large, our public schools have accepted the "philosophic compromise" interpretation of their function in a democracy. Under pressure from massive conflicting systems of interests and beliefs, they have agreed to agree to a politically expedient compromise "philosophy" which no one really believes and which parallels to a large extent the "balance of power" within our broader political institutions. The progressives, too, whose instinct derives (let us say, for now) from a passionately held set of beliefs about what is of value in human experience, have accepted this interpretation of democratic compromise. And because they have accepted it, they have had to be content with reactive rhetoric. The vision of the school that lies behind their rhetoric does not fit into the compromise.

It is a radical vision (as democracy is still a radical and unaccomplished vision) in the eye of a man who has agreed to a conservative compromise. So the best he can do is not to create but rather to settle for a rhetoric aimed at patching a little humanization onto a system that contradicts his notion of humanity. From this perspective, the continued publication of books and pamphlets telling us how to "humanize the schools" is a futile pastime. So we look for alternatives.

The alternative I would like to propose depends on a rejection of the continuing philosophic compromise. It recognizes that this compromise is a political stalemate rather than a philosophic truth, and that, consequently, it can be and is to be struggled against politically.

In place of Tyler's nonsensical assumption that the schools operate upon the basis of an "agreed upon philosophy," the alternative assumes that the school itself is an open battleground wherein two interdependent battles are fought: (a) it is the place where competing interests, political visions, ideologies, and value systems *external* to the school system itself struggle for control of society through the training of the young; and (b) it is the place where the young struggle to integrate private experience, social experience, and technical and symbolic experience into a way of being in the world, and at the heart of that struggle is the struggle with conflicting "philosophies."

The first corollary of this alternative assumption is a radical view of the curriculum worker. Instead of being a neutral exponent of a political compromise passing for a "philosophical agreement," he is seen as a partisan of an educational point of view that is in distinct conflict with that political compromise. And that point of view, in its simplest essence, is that school is a place where philosophies emerge out of experience rather than a place where experience is selected to serve an externally determined and politically motivated "philosophy." It sees, if you will, a dialectical rather than a mechanistic relation between the ends and means of education, and in this it is quite Deweyan. It holds that "objectives" emerge in experience and that simultaneously experience is guided by emergent objectives.

The discussion thus far suggests three main points to keep in mind about the situation of the progressively inclined curriculum worker:

1. The ineffectuality of the current movement to "humanize" education derives largely from its acceptance of the political compromise which passes for an "agreed upon philosophy."

2. The curriculum worker can redefine his role by deciding not to accept the political compromise. He can become a partisan of a point of view about education which lies outside of that compromise. He can define himself as a dissenter, as a member of an opposition party. He can recognize that school policy is shaped by a balance of political power rather than by apperception of philosophic truths, and he therefore can begin to think about his own struggle in terms of power.

3. The educational point of view of which he is a partisan is an opposition point of view not because it advocates this rather than that "philosophic agreement" as a basis for determining the objectives of the curriculum, but rather because it rejects per se the notion that objecives are to be derived at all from prior "philosophic agree-

ment." The relation between the ends and means of schooling is dialectical and not mechanical, and the business of schools is to provide the conditions under which that dialectic can proceed.

THE HEART OF HIGH SCHOOL STUDENT PROTEST

My premise in this section is as follows: At the heart of high school protest is the student's rage against being exploited, in the name of education, for purposes that are extrinsic to and independent of his own needs, interests, experiences, and emergent purposes. The rage is intensified by the feeling that his needs are not unknown or unthought of but rather are systematically manipulated as a key strategy in the exploitation.

A corollary of this premise is that these same students seek an educative environment which is designed to cultivate what is emergent in them, which takes its purposes from their sense of purpose, which organizes experience around their struggle to find a way of being in the world.

The importance of this premise is obvious. It suggests that there is a substantial consonance of interests between the angry young student protester and the new partisan curriculum worker. The consonance exists on three points. First, the educational intent of the two groups is the same. This follows directly from my premise.

The students, of course, do not assert their intent in neo-Deweyan terms, but their language—it emphasizes "experience," "growth," "freedom to explore," "finding yourself," "intrinsic rewards," and it abhors "manipulation," "working for somebody else's goals," etc.—strongly suggests the commonality of intent I have posited.[1]

Second, the students in question have already rejected the great

---

[1] This assertion is based upon many hours of conversation with high school students in nonschool educational contexts; some of the conversation was systematically "observed," most of it carefully listened to.

philosophic compromise discussed in the preceding section and stand in varying degrees of readiness to struggle against it. They dissent, and stridently, from the school's notion that this sort of compromise, this balancing of powers, is "the democratic way." Their vision encompasses a more subtle notion of democracy than sheer balancing of political power, and many of them are prepared to act militantly in the political struggle for a more highly democratic dispensation of the school's role in society. Here, too, they seem to have seen what Dewey saw without having read Dewey, for they sense that democracy, like education *in* a democracy, is a dialectical thing; a setting for emergence, growth, change; a system of process in which means and ends continuously emerge, interact, and alter each other. The students in question, then, are themselves prepared to challenge, to struggle; and in this sense, too, they have much in common with the new partisan curriculum worker.

The third point of commonality is also a point of synthesis. Just as, in the Deweyan view, the ends and means of education are in continuous dialectical interaction, so, too, educative experience and political struggle are themselves in continuous dialectical interaction with each other. Each is informed and modified by the other, and each appears now as means and now as ends. The traditional liberal fear of mixing politics and education stems from the premise that ends and means are separate and that conniving politicians will *use* "education" as a means of achieving political ends instead of as a means of achieving the end of the "educated man."

The fear, I repeat, of *mixing* politics and education comes from the premise of *separating* means and ends. However, if we assume that means and ends are not separate, that educative experience and political struggle are inseparable facets of a dialectical process, then neither a particular static political situation nor a particular version of the "educated man" can be regarded as ends; nor can "education" be regarded as a means to these or any other ends. The object of the liberal's fear vanishes in the light of a dialectical view of the relation between educational experience and political struggle.

This point, that educational experience and political struggle are dialectically related, that both appear simultaneously as both means and ends, that both are continuously emergent, new, in motion, and that each depends continuously upon the other, is the third point of commonality between the student protester and the new partisan curriculum worker; and it illuminates, I hope, the importance of the critical premise stated previously.

THE POTENTIAL

The educative and political potential in the situation so far described can be understood in terms of an application of the Deweyan outlook to an existing situation. The view put forth here assumes Dewey's doctrines of "interest" and "experience," and finds in student protest both an instance of preemptively intense interest and an occasion, potentially, for richly educative experience.

The important characteristics of the interest in question are as follows:

1. The ends and the means of the interest interact with each other in a complex way. The "end-in-view," to use Dewey's phrase, is a particular kind of educative experience. Achievement of that end-in-view depends in part upon alterations in the broader social milieu out of which school policy is formed. The means, however, encompass precisely that same kind of educative experience that is sought as an end-in-view, and the means also encompass changes in the broader social milieu upon which school policy depends. The interest, then, is dialectical. Means and ends, political and educational, merge into and emerge out of interactions in an experience which is "educational" in the Deweyan sense.

2. The interest, then, is in part an interest in a particular kind of process. The central characteristic of that process is interaction between students and environment in which *both* will be changed in directions about which some things are known but some other things are *not* known. The key thing that *is* known is that the direction of change is such

that the process of interaction itself is enriched and amplified, and its substance controlled by emergent end-in-view.

3. The centrality of process, however, does not preclude a variety of substantive dimensions entering into the students' interest. While specific substance is emergent and thus indeterminate, likely areas of substantive interest can be projected:

   a. There are concrete educational policies and practices which are regarded as standing in the way of the sort of educative experience the student seeks. The ability to identify and analyze these is likely to emerge as an area of interest.

   b. There is the need for alternative concrete educational policies and practices which will facilitate the sort of educative experience the student seeks. Students are likely to become interested in acquiring the ability to generate such policies and practices.

   c. There is the need to understand the relations between educational policy and practice and broader social and political phenomena.

   d. There is the need to be able to plan activities that will alter the educational-political environment in predictable ways. Characteristics of this environment and of its change properties are of substantive interest to the students.

4. In addition to the focus upon a dialectical process and in addition to substantive dimensions to the interest in question, there is the dimension of action. There is the need to act—to interact with the environment. This need is of paramount importance. The entire dialectical process by which means and ends, politics and education, student and environment interact and *affect* each other depends upon there being actual, real action in the world. This is not and cannot be a laboratory experiment or a controlled educative device. Without the actuality of action upon the environment of a sort that is largely indeterminate prior to the emergence of specific situations

calling for action, the preemptive interest is being exploited but not served, and the entire dynamic of this proposal ceases to function.

5. Because both theoretically and practically the policy of schools is determined in the context of broader political institutions, and because philosophically educative experience is part of and not apart from finding one's way in the world, it is in the interest of the students to regard the traditionally rigid and impermeable boundary between school and society as movable, flexible, permeable, and ultimately expendable.

THE OUTLINE OF A CURRICULAR RESPONSE

On the basis of this understanding of the educative potential of student protest, I can suggest a very general outline of an appropriate curricular response. The response mixes politics and education quite freely, for its premise is that they *are* mixed. It posits an alliance between partisan educators and struggling students, and thereby projects a new role for the curriculum worker—one in which his commitment to establish institutions is diminished and his commitment to education becomes properly dominant. It constitutes, I repeat, an application of Deweyan theory, and finds in student protest an instance of preemptively intense interest. This last point bears repetition. If it can once be understood that protest, no matter how one may view some particular form it takes, is an indicator of interest of the most pertinent sort, then the remainder of what I have to say will be simple and clear. The main dimensions of curricular response are represented in Figure 1.[2]

Action, it will be noted, is at the center. The arrows between the action center and the external points go in both direction. Ac-

[2] The points in this diagram must not be taken to represent "courses" or their equivalent. They are aspects of a dialectical whole, and there are a large number of ways of managing things such that all these aspects are incorporated in the student's experience. The "best" way depends upon local circumstances.

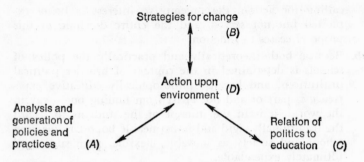

FIGURE 1   Dimensions of Curricular Response

tion provides an opportunity for the integration, application, and testing of knowledge acquired in connection with the external points. The interactions involved in action generate new data and new problems. All of the aims of any given action are "ends-in-view" which take their meaning from a broader framework and which yield dialectically to new emergent ends-in-views; and the action, while altering the environment, also leads back outward to the formulation of new inquiries, new knowledge, and back in again to new experience.

Following are some brief examples of specific kinds of content that may be found at each of the external points (A, B, C) in my diagram.

Point A. Analysis and Generation of Educational Policies and Practices

1. ANALYSIS. There are a variety of very concrete school practices and policies that students regard as inconsistent with and detrimental to their educational interests. These range from dress codes to grading systems, from censorship to writing assignments, from rules governing convening of meetings to rules governing access to information housed in the library. The students are sometimes correct and sometimes incorrect in their view that a given practice is detrimental to their educational interest. For the most part, however,

students are uniformly inexperienced in determining the intended function of the practice, its history, its component parts, its relation to alternative practices, etc. Consequently, even when their adverse judgment upon a given practice is correct, their ability to argue persuasively and act effectively is hampered.

With respect to "grading," for example, it is not uncommon to find two groups of students in dissent, on similar grounds, from current practice, to be fighting for conflicting alternatives, *neither of which actually removes the abuse involved in the initial practice.* Thus students may argue over tests or papers as a basis for grades without recognizing (a) that their very debate is conditioned by their tacit acceptance of certain assumptions concerning what attributes are to be evaluated by whom in reference to which criteria for what purpose, and (b) that their common grievance is with precisely these tacit assumptions.

The *analysis* part of point A, then, posits systematic analysis of whichever actual policies and practices are of most interest to the students in question. The analysis in particular would seek to disclose fundamental assumptions subtending policy and practice.[3]

2. GENERATION. If the analysis of practice leads to disclosure of fundamental assumptions, the converse is also true. Fundamental assumptions have the capacity to generate educative policy and practice. A conplementary process to the analytic one just described, then, is the identification by the student of fundamental propositions that express his commitments, beliefs, and understandings, and the generation of educative programs from these. Such propositions may be either discovered or invented—discovered in anything from the Pentateuch to the New Testament to Marx or Marcuse or Abbie Hoffman, or invented through one's own speaking and writing.

Many students, for example, speak a language of "experience" and "intrinsic value" and "growth" that reflects a system of belief not unlike that of John Dewey, who used similar language. Yet

---

[3] Again, this type of "analysis" is not intended to be treated as "subject matter" in a course.

these same students will frequently bypass this language, with all its implied assumptions, and attempt to develop their ideas about education through the use of a language like that of behavioral learning theory, which is built upon assumptions quite alien to their own.

The tool to be developed here is the practice of using the language that best expresses one's beliefs and values as the medium for generating appropriate educative programs. To return to the example of "grades," the student who is frustrated in his effort to deal with "grades" through the language and assumptions of learning theory may well be able to generate a cogent and satisfying approach to evaluation through a language that satisfies his own system of values and beliefs.

The two processes, analytic and generative, clearly interact in much the same way that "induction" and "deduction" or "analysis" and "synthesis" do. The creation, criticism, modification, destruction, and re-creation of appropriate educative environments reflect the dialectical relation between the processes. One discovers that the debate over grades is structured and constrained by a set of assumptions, and one discovers that an alternative set of assumptions generates an entirely different approach to the problem of evaluation.

Point B. Strategies for Change

Change in a direction about which only certain things are known is simultaneously the means and the ends of the whole show. Explicit attention to the problem of change is accordingly a subtle and complex thing. What is sought as an end-in-view is an educative situation which continuously generates the requisite conditions for the kind of change being sought. Bringing about such a situation in itself constitutes "changing" things. Response to this situation constitutes the dividing line between liberal and revolutionist methodology.

The liberals believe that you can bring about a given desired situation only by methods which adhere to the principles inherent in the desired situation. The revolutionists believe that an inherent characteristic of the situation to be changed is its unresponsiveness to change strategies governed by principles derived from a view of how things *should* be. The interplay between these views is complex, enormously important historically, and literally a matter of life and death in contemporary affairs.[4] Accompanied by varying degrees of awareness, this same interplay works itself broadly and deeply into the lives of today's dissident students. Thus it provides the basic paradigm for explicit consideration of strategies for change.[5]

Interest in change of any particular sort leads to a variety of more specific kinds of inquiries, too. One would like to seek answers to questions such as the following:

1. How does school policy actually come about, both in general and here at *this* school?

2. What alignments and balances of power give current practices their inertia?

3. Can these alignments and balances be analyzed into component parts which might be separately affected?

4. What is the history of other efforts to change schools in a direction similar to that now contemplated?

5. What are the boundaries and what are the interactions between specifically educational and more broadly social, economic, and/or political interests contributing to school policies?

6. What are the established theoretical points of view regarding bringing about change (either with specific reference to education or with more general reference to society at large)?

---

[4] An interesting instance of the struggle between these viewpoints may be found in the debate between Leon Trotsky and John Dewey (1969). Neither writer is at his best here. Each reveals his characteristic weakness. Still, the basic point of contention is clear.

[5] This does not mean that the paradigm itself becomes the principal *content* of a course or its equivalent. It means that awareness of the paradigm directs one's inquiries in a variety of subtle ways.

7. What are the currently emergent points of view about changes implied in sources as diverse as government policy documents and the revolutionary press?

8. What useful analogies may be drawn between the student's situation in school and such other situations as, for example, the struggle of workers for the rights of collective bargaining?

9. What are the legal rights and what are the legal constraints that appertain both to those seeking the given change and those opposing it?

10. What are the precedents and justifications for, implications and consequences of, and compelling arguments for and against recourse to extralegal means of bringing about change? What is the relation between "legal" and "ethical" in this context?

11. What, in general, is the nature of political power? How does it work; how is it achieved and how denied?

12. What is the particular distribution of power at this school? What are the inherent advantages and disadvantages in opposition status?

Such questions may be generated indefinitely. They are not intended to constitute a list of topics for a course; rather, these or similar questions are likely to emerge out of, and efforts to answer them are likely to provide input into, the effort to actually plan and enact strategies for bringing about desired change.

Point C. Relation of Politics to Education

I asserted early in this paper that protest against school experience is primary and protest against political structures is secondary for the dissident student. While I believe this assertion to be true, in terms of the biography of students, it is not clear that it is true historically or politically. It is a commonplace observation that there are two revolutions going on, and that one is cultural and the other is political. These two revolutions correspond to the two views regarding the relative primacy of educative experience and political structure.

The cultural revolution asserts the view that experience can be modified directly, and that new political structures will emerge out of new qualities of experience. The political revolution asserts that while the quality of experience is the ultimate concern, it cannot be modified directly—rather it requires modification of the political and economic structures which govern the quality of experience. The interplay between these two points of view is the focal point of the dissident student's interest in the relation between education and politics. It suggests a variety of kinds of inquiry, of which the following two may be especially important:

1. What does one make of the fact that, historically, philosophies of education have frequently been derived from political philosophies? Plato established the chief precedent for this. Major figures like Locke, Hobbes, and Jefferson conform to that precedent. Dewey, interestingly enough, is the only major figure coming readily to mind who asserts the primacy of the philosophy of education per se; and even he, in the very same book in which the assertion occurs —*Democracy and Education*—seems still to derive his fundamental educational propositions from several postulates about "the good society" (1916).

Further, even the idealists of the progressive movement, whose aspirations are nicely summed up in George S. Counts' title *Dare the School Build a New Social Order?* (1932) and whose emphasis was ever upon the *intrinsic* worth of educative experience, seemed to be moved by some prior notion of the good society.

Do these historic precedents warrant the conclusion that a political view is necessarily prior to a position about education, or is there an alternative to the view that education is a means to a political end? Harking back to an earlier section of this chapter, is it possible that the problem is an artifact created by the analytic separation of ends and means; conversely, can the artifact (if the problem *is* an artifact) be removed by regarding education and politics each as both means and ends in a dialectical social process?

2. Given the kind of interest I have stipulated here, the *intellectual* inquiry just described is likely to be associated with a parallel *practical* one. What is the relation in practice between actual *political and economic* structures and events and actual *educational* structures and events? Does one precede the other? Does one cause the other? Are they mutually and simultaneously caused by some other structure? Are they simultaneously emergent in interaction with each other and with other forces?

There are some obvious instances which might be explored beyond the level of established clichés, such as the relation between Sputnik and the rise to prominence of new science curricula. There are broader phenomena, such as those studied by Raymond E. Callahan regarding the relation between school policy and the emergent business ethic of the first half of the 20th century (1962). There are questions like those examined by Lauter and Howe regarding the relation between the "tracking system" and fundamental socioeconomic structures in our society (1970). There is the question of the history of federal appropriations for education and the relation of these appropriations to basic political and economic policy. (Most such appropriations have come in combination with economic, political, or military legislation; for example, the National Defense Education Act, and Federal Land Grants Act.)

There is the relatively unexplored question of the relation between criteria for success in school and criteria for the success of our basic political and economic systems. At a more fundamental level still, there is the question of the relation between the assumptions about the nature of man and about what is valuable in human experience that are implied on the one hand in our basic economic and political institutions and on the other in our basic methodology for both the conduct of research and the conduct of practice in education.

All these questions arise in connection with the student's interest in the interplay, both within and around him, between the cultural and political revolutions. This interplay makes demands upon him. It is not, for him, a discrete intellectual exercise. He is in the process of making fundamental choices about his independent identity, and a most vital component of these choices is acceptance, in some measure, of responsibility toward the chaotic world he is finding he lives in. The demands made upon him are thus also demands he makes upon himself; they are demands made in light of the taking of responsibility, and consequently they are demands not only for understanding but for acting as well.

Thus the relation between politics and education examined in light of the interplay between the two revolutionary points of view interacts directly with the central point D of my diagram. The questions emerge out of a commitment to act upon the environment. The ideas shape the action; and, in action, concrete specific problems arise that reshape the inquiry. As in the previous sections, then, this discussion of the relation of politics to education is not intended to supply the content for a discrete course or unit. Course content in the abstract is indeterminate, unpredictable. It is shaped by emerging events. Discussion of the three external points (A, B, C) is intended to delineate a likely common scope of inquiries that will emerge, as interests of the sort I posited here are pursued in action. In pointing to this scope of inquiries, I intend only to imply that an appropriate curricular response to the students here being discussed includes *anticipation* of such inquiries and *preparation* to deal in some appropriate form with them, as they emerge.

THE CURRICULA RESPONSE CONTINUED— WHAT THE EDUCATOR CAN DO

I have attempted thus far to illuminate various aspects of the protesting student's educational interests, and to show how they coincide with the interests of the partisan curriculum worker. I have necessarily done so in a manner that leaves a variety of important questions untouched.[6]

---

[6] Among these the most important probably has to do with the relation between the student's protest, which I have argued is grounded in his *educational* experiences, and the broader, more specifically political revolutionary

What I would like to do now, in this final section, is to point a bit more specifically to the kinds of things the educator can do to build upon this coincidence of interests. I will begin with two working assumptions:

1. High school students will continue to protest against school systems which are essentially oppressive and inflexible. The number of such students will grow. Their protest will be increasingly more active and more militant. Their tactics will include the following: holding meetings, leafleting, publishing newspapers, picketing, boycotting, forming alliances with other groups, petitioning, using mass media, engaging in acts of civil disobedience, bringing court suits on behalf of constitutionally protected civil rights.

2. Because educative political experience has been systematically excluded from their education, students will continue to express their legitimate grievances in ways which are often politically incoherent and ineffective. Because students have been systematically excluded from serious active participation in the analysis of educational problems and the generation of practices that respond to their needs, they will continue to miss the point, often, in their efforts to identify the problems and to generate solutions.

There are three very unfortunate consequences of this situation. First, the student movement will be much less effective in accomplishing laudable ends than it might otherwise be. Second, the ineffectiveness of the actions, aside from being unfortunate in itself, strengthens the tendency of school systems to seek to isolate such actions from any serious political, educational, or intellectual context so that they may more readily be handled as simple, vacuous

---

tendencies which are developing among non-student sectors of the population. This question I will have to leave untouched for now, except to point out the likelihood that the relation will crystallize as students, with the support of educators, seek to integrate their formal educational experience with their present life-situations.

misbehaviors, and this response predictably leads to a series of esca-
lations in hostility. Third, the actions will tend to fall short of their
potential as integrative centers for the educational and political
process I have described.[7]

Given the situation, there are at least three fairly obvious
strategic goals in terms of which a productive alliance between the
student and the curriculum worker may be built. First, the curriculum worker can help to develop political support for the particular
objectives of the particular group of students in question at a particular time. He can do this both within a school and outside in
the broader community to which the school is responsible. A critical
part of this task is developing a context in terms of which the objectives of the students can be *understood* by other members of the
community (Mann, 1970). This is critical precisely because, as previously noted, the tendency of schools is to overcome opposition by
isolating its objectives from the contexts required to make them
comprehensible.

The success of this strategy is augmented, I think, by a common tendency of the students themselves to develop a kind of de-
fensive disdain for people who do not immediately comprehend the
entire value system implicit in some small gesture of theirs. And this
leads directly into the second strategic goal. Active and serious support on behalf of the students' objectives is a proper and necessary
prerequisite to the sort of confidence required for access to the intellectual and emotional processes of the students' actions.

The second strategic goal is to use that access to push continuously for a clarification of objectives, for a broadening context in
which to place the objectives, and, thereby, for the kind of fluidity
of mind which allows given objectives to function as ends-in-view
or as "transitional demands" rather than as fixed ends. This is critical politically and educationally:

---

[7] It is interesting, though, to note the great number of successful instances of students' breaking from established school systems to form their own
educational-political cooperatives. In some of these, the quality of the total
educational-political experience is astonishingly good.

1. Because without it the educator's effort to develop a context through which the community may view student protest has no grounding in interaction with the students and is thus likely to become increasingly untrustworthy;

2. Because without such fluidity, without the capacity to see and use goals transitionally, the educational and political processes become frozen, bogged down in standoffs, with the almost certain result that violence escalates and the established powers win their point and discredit the opposition in the process; and (most important)

3. Because it is in this context that many students who have previously accepted the school view of learning—that it is a discrete process separated by layers of physical and psychological concrete from personal and social needs, commitments, and interests—will begin to discover the full force of the alternative they have been seeking to establish. This discovery in turn contributes to a clarification of the educational goals being sought through a political process and helps thereby to confirm the dialectical character of the entire process under discussion. It is in the context of this second strategic goal—the clarification of objectives and the broadening of contexts—that the external points A, B, C of the diagram on page 164 explicitly enter the picture. For here the various inquiries suggested take on meaning in the light of active interests and commitments. And this proposition leads in turn to the third strategic goal.

The third strategic goal is the establishment of centers—physical locations—to serve as home base for the educational-political experience. Obviously the people involved need a place to meet for such things as planning studies and actions, discussing common readings and experiences, and preparing materials. A "place" also serves a symbolic function for both members and nonmembers. It gives a spatial and concrete dimension to an entity which without location has a necessarily amorphous quality.

A place also serves as a center for communication. Without a center for communication it is almost impossible to develop effective political opposition. That is why our Constitution, in guaranteeing the right to oppose, deals so explicitly with the various forms of communication (speech, assembly, press, petition), and this is why the key political issue in high schools today is precisely the issue of the student's right to freedom of speech, assembly, press, and petition. Before any other issue is launched, one has to make one's concerns and beliefs and analyses known.

Finally, a place serves an expressly political purpose because in a place a number of individuals becomes an entity, an alternative institution with not only a number of people in it but also a *way* of going about things. And this in-corporation (putting into a body) of the principles for which the group stands gives an objective dimension to the enterprise. And this objective dimension, the collectivity, adds important information to what otherwise is a personality-centered view available to interested people who might wish to support the programs at one or another level. It also adds a kind of objective correlative to the subjective view of those within the group, and this serves as a useful basis for self-critique.

The actual location of a place, the kind of place it is, and the way it functions will vary vastly with circumstances. It should be a place where people go after school, or during school at selected times, or, for some people, instead of school. Its strategy involves continually expanding interaction with individual schools and with school systems. It seeks to legitimize its existence as an alternative to established schools, and its practices as an alternative to established practices, both within those established schools and within the broader community. It may attempt test cases taken to the school board or the courts involving the right of an individual student to meet a portion of his state's education requirement by participation at the center in vital educative experiences not offered at the established school.

These three strategic goals—development of political support, broadening intellectual foundations, and assistance in the establishment and effective functioning of a center away from school—open the way to substantial mutually supportive interaction between students and professional educators. A variety of other strategies are possible, and I have barely scratched the surface of possible tactics within each of these strategies.

In the preceding pages I have done two things. First, I have provided a view of contemporary high school student protest which establishes a close kinship between the aspirations of students and the fundamental intent of certain educators whose roots are in the progressive conception of education. Second, I have given the outline, at both a theoretical and an applied level, of an appropriate curricular response to high school student protest. The key point in the analysis of protest is the assertion that it is fundamentally an expression of dismay and disgust with the failure of established schooling practices to correspond at all to the student's emerging thoughts, beliefs, commitments, values, interests, perceptions, and needs. In the student's eye and in mine this failure reflects a broader social and political failure of other fundamental institutions. The corrective involves not only the espousal of good ideas but also the development of sufficient political force. The political struggle the students are involved in to achieve a better education system is, or can be, an exemplary educative situation itself as well as an effective political force.

The appropriate progressive curricular response to this situation is the formation of an alliance between educator and student through which the educator can (a) cultivate public understanding and support for the vision of education he shares with the students, both as a context for current student "unrest" and as a programmatic direction for our educational institutions; (b) help students become politically more effective by broadening the intellectual base of their protest with respect to educational and political theory and practice; and (c) help assure that the educative potential present in a group of young people acting upon deeply felt commitment is realized as fully as possible in the experience of political struggle, both because of the intrinsic worth of this experience and because of the capacity of such experience to deepen the students' understanding of what they seek in the first place.

Much of this discussion is incomplete. Its virtue is that it takes student protest as serious and projects a serious way for an educator to respond. Taking protest as a discipline problem with no substantive educational or political content is a commoner way but a futile, stupid, and wasteful way to respond. An acceptable response must at least meet the requirement that it discover educational potential in the dismay, anger, aspiration, and commitment that enter into protest.

REFERENCES

RAYMOND E. CALLAHAN. *Education and the Cult of Efficiency.* Chicago: University of Chicago Press, 1962.

GEORGE S. COUNTS. *Dare the School Build a New Social Order?* New York: The John Day Company, Inc., 1932.

JOHN DEWEY. *Democracy and Education.* New York: The Macmillan Company, 1916.

PAUL LAUTER and FLORENCE E. HOWE. *Conspiracy of the Young.* New York: The World Publishing Company, 1970.

JOHN S. MANN. *"Political Power and the High School Curriculum." Educational Leadership* 28 (1): 23–26; October 1970.

LEON TROTSKY and JOHN DEWEY. *Our Morals and Theirs.* New York: Pathfinder Press, 1969.

RALPH TYLER. *Basic Principles of Curriculum and Instruction.* Chicago: University of Chicago Press, 1949.

ROBERT PAUL WOLFF, BARRINGTON MOORE, JR., and HERBERT MARCUSE. *A Critique of Pure Tolerance.* Boston: Beacon Press, 1965.

10

COMMUNICATION:
A Curriculum Focus

MARGARET AMMONS

Margaret Ammons' article is a direct response to a request for a new way to focus the curriculum. For this reason she is particularly aware of the need to lay out her ideas in a straightforward manner and to justify her position on the curriculum.

Though her focus is on a single process in contrast to Berman (Chapter 11), the reader will note that Ammons' definitions and concerns are broadly conceived. She is concerned with verbal and non-verbal communication, cognitive, psychomotor, and affective behavior, and the mode of instruction most appropriate to her communication focus. She explicitly rejects the single- and multi-discipline alternatives available to curriculum workers. In this light it is well to compare Ammons with King and Brownell (Chapter 5) and Bellack (Chapter 6).

For Ammons, communicating is an essential, persistent process that each person must use throughout his entire life. (Compare this with Stratemeyer's persistent life situations presented in Chapter 3.) Yet Ammons claims that "communication may be one of the activities in which we engage with the least skill." Is she correct? If so, does this justify her focus on communication?

Let's put it another way. Ammons claims that communication is a "legitimate core" around which to plan a curriculum. The reader, after carefully considering her assumptions, facts, and conclusions, must ask if her communication focus is adequate and sufficient. To answer this it is well to compare Ammons with Berman (Chapter 11) and Stratemeyer (Chapter 3).

<><><><><><><><><><><><><><><><><><><><><><><><><><><><><>

Given the charge of preparing an example of a new way to organize a curriculum for children, I have found my paper falling into what seems to me to be four natural sections. Three of these are in essence a foundation for the fourth, the proposal of a new curriculum design focused on communication. The paper opens with some remarks that provide general background, after which I define key terms and then proceed to spell out the basic assumptions on which the design proposal itself rests.

In any one of the sections you must recognize that much of what is set down is sheer assertion or assumption, although I may sometimes neglect to identify for the reader just where this is so. I defend myself in this regard on the grounds that where curriculum, as defined here, is concerned, we have little other than organized assumptions to go on. Therefore, I will try to present as tight a case for what I propose as I am able to do, believing firmly that in our present stage of professional development, there is no viable alternative to our doing so. Hopefully, this reasoning will be exonerated by the end of the paper.

GENERAL BACKGROUND

My first assertion is that "The elementary school as we know it is largely the product of historical accidents." That is to say, the graded school for children roughly five or six to eleven or twelve years of age was not a result of national studies or assessment, nor careful experiments regarding child growth and development, nor an adoption or revision of what knowledge is of most worth, nor surveys to determine the most pressing needs of children in the given age bracket. I need not here catalogue the critical dates of the history of the elementary school in its entirety. Most assuredly, some few changes have occurred. The changes, however, were again not the result of the kind of thoughtful inquiry and introspection to which we would be pleased to admit. Rather, decisions regarding the elementary school have been made in response to such questions as "What will we do with rapidly increasing numbers of children?" And thus grades. Then, "What will be studied in each of these grades?" Thus graded textbooks and graded teachers. Not one of such decisions or answers was responsive to searching questions which, to me at least, appear relevant to children.

Given such decisions, we have then attempted to justify them after the fact, as in the following statement: "The best basic unit of organization yet devised is the self-contained classroom in which a group of children of similar social maturity are grouped together under the extended and continuous guidance of a single teacher." This statement was published originally in 1950 and quoted in

1960.[1] At the time of either publication, there were no other basic units of organization in sufficient numbers to have made a thoroughgoing comparative study which would have allowed such an assertion to be made.

Furthermore, programs established on such bases as described above have been maintained *in essence* in spite of data which point to something other than the present elementary school program and organization. Perhaps most critical, however, is that while we have tinkered with such elements as flexible buildings, team teaching, computers, nongrading, and so on, the curriculum has remained in essence the same.

To repeat: the curriculum, or in general those things which have been proffered to children to learn, has not changed in essence. By essence, I mean simply that, when the trimmings have been peeled away, what remains as the core around which the curriculum is built has remained unaltered for decades. One piece of evidence for this is a number of studies conducted in response to charges that schools of the 'fifties were not doing as well as schools of the earlier part of this century. In spite of the fact that we claimed to be doing something different, in which case we should simply have said, "You're right, we're not trying to do the same thing," we hastened to haul out tests which would, for example, measure in 1953 what the tests were initially designed to measure in 1933. If there is no difference between 1933 results and 1953 results on tests designed to measure 1933 performances, it would appear on the surface that whatever happened to children in 1953 was at least similar to what happened in 1933; that is, what happened to them in terms of learning opportunities.[2]

Let me put it in another way. Once upon a time we were faced with the task of making members of our society literate. Initially, this meant teaching the three R's. Slowly literacy came to be defined

---

[1] Association for Supervision and Curriculum Development. *The Self-Contained Classroom*. Washington, D.C.: the Association, 1960.

[2] V. V. Miller and W. C. Lanton. "Reading Achievement of School Children—Then and Now." *Elementary English* 33: 91–97; February 1956.

to include in addition the possession of certain information, social science information, for example. That is, subject matter "mastery" somehow came to be equated with success and literacy. Obviously, the school was the place where such mastery should occur.

Supposedly, however, our expressed purpose now is somewhat different from mere literacy. We speak of producing persons who possess such attributes as critical thinking, or analytical abilities, or abilities to sort out fact from fiction, or appreciation of the humanities. Yet the studies we have available reveal at least two unsettling generalizations about what transpires in elementary classrooms. First, teacher classroom behavior is determined more by textbooks than by any other single factor.[3] Second, approximately 90 percent of teachers' questions require no more of the learner than that he recall some specific piece of information or that he be able to put someone else's idea into his own words.[4]

The point is this: Despite aspirations and claims to the contrary, what actually happens in elementary classrooms, at least in large numbers of them, puts a ceiling on what children are expected to do. And ceilings are placed in the traditional subject areas. When children are given grades, they are typically evaluated in terms of performance in subject areas. Some attention is given to such other factors as the quality of their citizenship and their effort; but these are often judged as children function in subject areas. Furthermore, a rapid survey of statutory requirements regarding the elementary school program reveals that these are typically set down in terms of subject matter to be taught and amount of time to be spent per week on certain areas.

Thus, mastery of subject matter or literacy is still the operational goal in elementary education. Earlier, the expressed goal and

---

[3] D. Gilmore. "A Critical Examination of Selected Instructional Practices." Unpublished doctoral dissertation. East Lansing: Michigan State University, 1963.

[4] F. J. Guszak. "A Study of Teacher Solicitation and Student Response Interaction About Reading Content in Selected Second, Fourth, and Sixth Grades." Unpublished doctoral dissertation. Madison: University of Wisconsin, 1966.

the operational goal were the same and a program appropriate for their attainment was developed. Now there is a basic discrepancy between expressed and operational goals; the program is reflective of the operational, not the expressed goal. The reasons for this situation constitute an interesting problem for exploration, but such explorations are beyond the limits of this paper.

Thus while we want to change, while we alter school organization, we still divide the child's school world into the same subject areas which have been the basis for schooling for decades. Furthermore, with such notable exceptions as the work of Suchman, new projects have been developed within the framework of disciplines or academic specialties. The apparent objective in some such projects has been to make better mathematicians of elementary school children, or better scientists, or better historians, or better users of the mother tongue.

The question which cries for thoughtful consideration is whether the goal of the elementary school is to prepare young children for more adequate performance in the academic disciplines at later educational stages by earlier and earlier concentration on the disciplines—or whether the purpose of the elementary school is something quite different. While this question will be dealt with in some detail at a later point, let me assert now my own position— the purpose of the elementary school is *not* to create academicians at earlier and earlier ages.

DEFINITIONS

Let us turn now to the definition of some terms which will recur and upon the definition of which much of what is to follow hangs. There are five such terms: curriculum, instruction, communication, objectives, and evaluation.

By *curriculum* I mean an educational plan which includes a statement of objectives, a description of exemplary learning situations, and a description of exemplary evaluation techniques, the latter two designed in relation to objectives. This plan is drawn for a group of learners for whom the planners have responsibility, as, for example, all the children in a school district.

Instruction in this context is defined as the interaction between teacher and pupil or pupils which is intended to assist the learner toward the achievement of specified objectives.

Communication here is a rather simple concept. It is not burdened with the theoretical constructs of communications specialists, though such specialists have much to contribute. Here communication is defined as a two-way process in which one individual intends that a particular meaning be grasped by another or others, and in which others grasp the intended meaning. I acknowledge that the word "meaning" is fraught with ambiguity and various philosophical and psychological over- and undertones. But if I were to use the word "message," I would be in similar difficulty. When I use the word communication, I hope the reader will decode it with the same interpretation that I place upon it.

Objectives are statements of purpose which describe the desired student behavior and the content in relation to which the student is to behave. Objectives have as their function guiding, not dictating to, teachers in selecting appropriate learning situations and evaluation techniques. Parenthetically, both behavior and content are conceived of here in very broad terms.

Evaluation is intended to mean a description of an individual's progress toward one or more objectives. So much for terms.

BASIC ASSUMPTIONS

There is a set of assumptions which I make about the nature of man, the knowable, the good society, and man's relation to it. From these, hopefully, grow some assumptions which relate directly to elementary education.

First, man is rational. By this I mean that man can see alternatives and choose among them. Further, in my frame of reference, rationality in man means that man does not act capriciously, whimsically, or without some justification which to him makes sense; that is, man behaves with reason. Even further, man can learn to increase his ability to act with reason, to improve through his own power his grounds for choosing. Man desires to improve, has the courage to improve, is curious and enthusiastic about things which have meaning for him. And finally, man is a social animal, requiring direct and vicarious human contact and response for survival. If I did not hold this belief, I would have little purpose in teaching.

Second, I assume that much is knowable which cannot be accounted for through the perception of the senses. I can know what it is like to be lonely or happy, but I know this in a way that is probably different from the way I know that something is blue, or hard, or sweet, or true, or harmonious. If this is so, then what I offer to a learner to know must include knowing in many ways. Knowledge cannot be limited to what is measured by responses to a paper and pencil test. What I accept as knowledge, and therefore knowable, must allow for empathic knowing, for sensitivity to another's perceptions of occurrences. It means that much of worth is known without my intervention or awareness. Learners do come to know without me. I assume that knowledge and knowing are a means, not an end. Finally, knowing, and thus learning, is deeply personal for each individual.

The good society is one in which man is free to choose, to make of himself what he will, to participate in the business of living according to his own lights. Such a society encourages independence of mind and spirit and does not bend humankind to its own ends, however magnanimous these may be. It is a society which provides the context for freedom of choice of the individual. The individual, in turn, has the obligation to behave as a human being, with the capacity for reasoning and choosing, with the ability to add to his store of knowledge whatever will allow him to become what he potentially is and to contribute to the good of all. It is a society which exists for the individual as he lives with others, not one for which the individual exists. It accords to the individual the ability to make his own rational and informed decisions.

The foregoing statements represent only a brief summary of where I stand on the questions which each of us must answer for himself as he contemplates the task of educating the young. If I am able to be consistent, these assumptions, or this value position, if you prefer, would seem to give rise to some further assumptions regarding elementary education:

1. The purpose of elementary schools is not to prepare a child for "a" or "the" next step in the sense of "getting him ready" for first grade or sixth grade, or high school, or college.

2. The best preparation for "next steps" is success at tasks which are valuable and relevant to a learner wherever he is.

3. Instruction and the plans for it derive or should derive from the curriculum of a particular school system or district.

4. Schools must define their curricula in terms of something which hopefully is relevant to the elementary child as he is.

5. Performing is different from learning. Performing is a short-lived change in behavior displayed in order to meet some external standard; learning is a persistent change in behavior displayed because the individual has "internalized" a new way of behaving or because he values it sufficiently to make it characteristic of his behavior patterns.[5]

6. Currently in elementary education, as elsewhere, we emphasize performance rather than learning.

7. Possession of information does not guarantee a permanent change in behavior.

8. The study of academic subject matter for its own sake does not guarantee an "educated" individual or one who has learned.

9. Mastery of academic subject matter is currently the end of elementary education. Some evidence in support of this

---

[5] Margaret P. Ammons. "Do We Really Want Students to Learn?" *Oregon Foreign Language Newsletter,* October 1967.

assumption is the fact that success or failure is determined in part by this criterion.

10. Conditions are changing so radically and rapidly that educational needs of elementary children as defined in the past are no longer relevant.

11. Academic subject matter can in fact become the means not the end of education.

12. Academic subject matter can be justified in the curriculum as it contributes to the individual's ability to communicate.

13. To change the essence of the elementary curriculum, we must alter our pattern of thinking and talking about the elementary curriculum.

14. As long as we segment the elementary program without some unifying theme, we deny what many assert to be true in the lives of human beings, namely the need to see the world as a whole piece.

15. Given such conditions, I am willing to put my money on communication as relevant at any point in a human's life.

A COMMUNICATIONS CURRICULUM

Given the foregoing rationale, what follows is a justification for a curriculum or the skeleton of a curriculum that I would propose as being more responsive to the child and his real world. The questions whose answers suggest or at least allow this curriculum are perhaps more important than the program itself. The curriculum proposal to follow is an illustration of a process in application more than it is a full-blown description of a program. Many of the questions it tries to answer have already been identified or implied.

Justification

Earlier I have denied either implicitly or explicitly that simple literacy is an acceptable purpose if it is the main or only purpose. I have also rejected the purpose of elementary education as that of preparing an individual for any next stage of education. Let me again disavow the notion of some that the purpose of elementary education is to teach children to think as does a scientist, a mathematician, or any other scholar in any other discipline.

The reasons for such rejections are probably obvious from what has been said to date. Let me here state some of these reasons briefly. I reject literacy as the end of education because it restricts the view held by the child of himself and his world. I reject preparation for next stages because in the main any stage of education has been artificially and arbitrarily determined; thus such preparation is also artificial and arbitrary. I reject the purpose of having children think as does a scholar because at the level of the elementary child, it is presumptuous to pretend that he is, in any real sense, capable of such activity. To assume that one child can think in the pattern of scholars in some seven to nine different fields is unrealistic and perhaps undesirable.

To try to force a child to choose a discipline of special interest at the elementary level, which might be an alternative, is to violate several of my basic assumptions. It would deny him the opportunity to become sufficiently acquainted with his world so that his choice would be informed and suitable. Inherent is the danger that the choice will be made for him in relation to something other than his individual welfare. Furthermore, to place such emphasis upon the disciplines is to make them become ends in themselves rather than means to be used by individuals for their own ends.

From these assertions an acceptable purpose of elementary education seems to me to emerge. In its broadest terms, the purpose of elementary education is to assist the individual child to cope with the world as he finds it. Such coping involves understanding, a major part of which is to be able to interpret accurately the stimuli he receives from his world. Here I include stimuli to the emotional or affective "senses."

More specifically, the purpose of elementary education is to help the child acquire the attitudes and skills he needs to interpret his world and to clarify for himself what the implications for him and for his own choices might be. As a child, it is more important for him to understand his world in his own terms than to behave in the mode of a scholar in any one or all of the disciplines. The term I have chosen for this kind of interpretation is communication.

My focus on the child's ability to communicate rests upon these facts: (a) communication is essential to both communal and individual living; (b) communication may be one of the activities in which we engage with the least skill;[6] and (c) maintenance of the fabric of our own society may be dependent upon communication. On this last point, for example, Richard Sanger suggests that one factor which may affect what happens in the expression of political feeling, whether it becomes violent or not, is the gap in communications between the ruling group and the discontented.[7]

Further, given individual differences, it seems likely that each of us may communicate effectively in only a small number of media, meaning by media language, body movement, painting, and the like. For example, when some 110 children were asked how many different ways they could think of to help someone understand what they meant, almost without exception they relied upon words as the medium. My own belief is that we fail to exploit many media as means of communication, thus reducing the possibilities for any one individual to choose the medium most appropriate for him and the particular message he is intent upon sending or receiving.

In any case, I view communication as a legitimate core around which to plan the program of the elementary school so that areas of study may contribute to the child's ability to cope with his world on his own terms. These areas of study—reading, mathematics, social sciences, the arts—can thus become functional as means rather than as ends. If we speak of the needs of children as a factor in organizing the elementary school, we may concede that one need to which the school can turn its attention in a unique fashion is communication; for it would appear that the elementary school is

---

[6] Ladislas Farago. *The Broken Seal*. New York: Random House, Inc., 1967.

[7] "Is Insurrection Brewing in U.S.?" Interview with Richard H. Sanger. *U.S. News and World Report* 63: 32–37; December 25, 1967.

the agency which can utilize the "disciplines" in helping children to sharpen their communication. Since communication appears to be a need which will exist as far into the future as I care to predict, and a need which exists at any level of development, I am willing to posit this area as the basis for organizing the elementary program.

With such an overall purpose, I would hope each child would be given the opportunity to:

1. Experience real communication with peers and with representatives of the appropriate academic disciplines
2. Participate in activities in which communication is essential to the individual in acquiring what he wants
3. Explore a variety of ways and means for getting messages across to others, particularly ways which he has not explored heretofore
4. Examine what ideas may most appropriately be communicated through the language of the different disciplines
5. Conversely, examine the role of mathematics, drama, and music in communication
6. Interpret the "messages" from the various disciplines and use such messages in making decisions about himself, his world, and his relation to it
7. Examine feelings, his own and those of others, to explore how these are communicated among humans and to comprehend the effects of feelings among humans
8. In general, increase sensitivity to his own communication as well as to the communication of others.

If these are at least some of the parameters of a curriculum with a communications focus, what comprises the substance? Time does not permit a detailed specification; however, I will list the objectives which I see as essential for elementary education, some description of organizing elements which bind the curriculum together, some illustrative activities, and several evaluation techniques which allow us to make some judgment regarding the progress of individual children.

Objectives

As I see it, there are four major objectives for the elementary school child: (a) that he be able to make reasoned and wise choices regarding his own behavior in a radically changing social context; (b) that he acquire the tools which allow such wise choices; (c) that he become increasingly independent in his learning; and (d) that he value learning as a means of coping with his world. Given what I believe regarding learning and the necessity for it to be a personal and individually internal affair, and given the definition I offered of communication, then communication is the key to the contribution which the elementary school can make to the individual child.

Elements

The organizing elements which run throughout the curriculum could be more clearly set forth with a diagram; however, let me try to construct a verbal diagram for you. Imagine a two by three table; that is, three columns and two rows, six cells. Across the top are three types of behavior; down the side are two types of activities.

Although there are many ways to categorize human behavior, e.g., Guilford or Gallagher-Aschner, I find the work of the committee of University Examiners and the home economics group at the University of Illinois the most useful and presently the most comprehensive. These groups have described human behavior as having three dimensions: cognitive, affective, and psychomotor. No claim is made that these are absolutely discrete, but rather that any given behavior is more of one type than of the other two. No claim is made either that these descriptions are final. In any case, they are helpful in talking about what is possible in terms of human behavior. So across the top of the diagram place these three terms.

One way to talk about the manner in which these behaviors are put into operation is modes of behavior. I am not fond of the term, but it is intended to distinguish between *types* of behavior and the way in which one *uses* each behavior. The modes which seem most appropriate in the present context are verbal and nonverbal. Down the side of the diagram, then, place those two words.

Given this arrangement, it is possible to talk about engaging in behavior in either a verbal or nonverbal way. Thus we may speak of verbal-cognitive behavior, verbal-affective behavior, verbal-psychomotor behavior, and nonverbal-affective behavior, nonverbal-cognitive behavior, and nonverbal-psychomotor behavior.

Thus we have the elements around which the program is to be built. The next major task is to determine what broad categories of schoolroom activities can be developed to allow the child to participate in the various types of communication and how they might be arranged both horizontally and vertically, a rather difficult consideration.

Organization

Recalling one of the major problems I now see with the program of the elementary school, it is incumbent upon me to suggest an alternative. The problem is fragmentation or splitting of the child's academic world into unrelated parts. Perhaps what I am about to suggest is simply another type of fragmentation, and I suspect that it is. Yet I believe the proposed approach exhibits more unity than do other plans and may serve at least to reduce the problem of fragmentation.

Over the years there have been various attempts to relate horizontally all the aspects of the elementary program. These attempts have included, among others, the integrated curriculum, the fused curriculum, and the core curriculum. The present proposed solution sounds similar to some aspects of each of these, but the intent is different. The intent is to relegate the disciplines to the level of tools rather than to consider these as something to be dealt with for their own sake. Some may interpret this as anti-intellectualism. Not so. I contend that the most intellectually respectable activity in which a child can engage is that of relating to his world in such a way that he can fulfill the objectives I set forth earlier. If independence in and love of learning are anti-intellectual, so be it.

Now what kind of horizontal organization makes sense for the elementary school child who is exposed to a curriculum built around communication? It is *not* relating or attempting to relate to communication the instructional areas as they are presently structured; that is, there is no concern with maintaining the present boundaries of the subject areas. If it should occur in the process that language arts, as this area is currently construed, is most useful in the form now taught, then it should be retained in that form. However, the major concern is that the program be organized so that children have opportunities to engage in verbal-cognitive behavior so that some aspects of language instruction would be essential. Such instruction, however, would be in relation to a type of communication rather than in relation to mastery of an area of study.

Another example of horizontal organization may be taken from mathematics. This field, of course, has significant impact upon the world of children. The contention here is that for the elementary school child, understanding the contribution of the various areas of scholarship to his own personal world is more appropriate than becoming a master of the field itself. Thus, learning what the mathematician has to say to the individual, learning how these ideas are expressed, and grasping the implications of mathematical ideas is to be emphasized.

Further, since nonverbal-cognitive behavior is one of the elements to be stressed throughout the curriculum, opportunities to wrestle with the area of nonverbal symbolism become relevant and crucial. To illustrate, and parenthetically I am not a numerologist, mathematical operations are not the only contribution made by the field. In Wisconsin I wager if one says the number 15 something exciting is communicated. Or if one is a Cub fan, then the number 14 is significant. One kind of communication is nonverbal-cognitive, and it seems that restricting children's exposure to the symbols typically associated with mathematics to the study of mathematics *qua* mathematics is limiting the opportunity of children to develop their sensitivity to the ideas communicated most appropriately through nonverbal symbols.

Another form of communication is nonverbal-affective. According to those who have tilled the field of affective behavior, this is the most neglected area in the schools. Yet many assert that unless and until the affect is involved, little learning of a permanent nature will occur.[8] If, then, we are concerned with the affective behavior of elementary school children, we must design the curriculum to account for such behavior. Since by definition communication of any kind necessarily involves the affect, nonverbal-affective behavior is legitimate and necessary. What this implies for the classroom is a study of the "silent language" described by Hall.[9] It involves work with ballet, pantomime, and other vehicles for communicating feelings to others. It involves offering children the chance to explore their own feelings, how they communicate these to others, and how they can be increasingly certain that they are accurately interpreting the feelings and messages of others.

When verbal-affective behavior is under consideration, we can turn to the general semanticists. A study done with sixth-grade children showed among other things that children of that age can deal with ideas in general semantics and that they find such involvement exciting. There is some reason to think that the materials used in that study could be adapted for younger children if this were desirable.

Looking, then, at horizontal organization, imagine a circle containing smaller, overlapping circles formed with broken lines. These six circles represent the six types of communication. You will recall the six: verbal-cognitive, verbal-affective, verbal-psychomotor, nonverbal-cognitive, nonverbal-affective, and nonverbal-psychomotor. The large circle represents a slice from the total curriculum, which may be thought of in this context as a cylinder. The area surrounding the six smaller circles contains the ideas from academic areas

---

[8] See: *Learning and Mental Health in the School.* Walter B. Waetjen and Robert R. Leeper, editors. Washington, D.C.: Association for Supervision and Curriculum Development, 1964; see particularly the chapter by: Donald Snygg. "A Cognitive Field Theory of Learning." pp. 77–96.

[9] E. T. Hall. *The Silent Language.* New York: Doubleday & Company, Inc., 1959.

I have mentioned, along with whatever additional ideas are needed to complete the curriculum. It should be noted that the smaller circles are composed of broken lines and are overlapping, suggesting that at least theoretically fragmentation is reduced and that appropriate aspects of areas of study feed directly into one or more types of communication, with the types of communication forming a whole.

Vertical, or overtime, organization of the curriculum requires a different approach. Whereas horizontal organization accounts for what we now call scope, vertical organization is concerned with sequence. Two major sets of ideas must be brought into relation in determining sequence. These are ideas from child development and ideas from areas of study. Please notice I have shifted terminology from discipline to areas of study. The reason is that we may be caught in the present trap of a disciplines curriculum if we persist adopting a discipline *in toto*. Rather we need to look to areas of study to determine what ideas from each area are relevant to the various types of communication.

At this point, I must remind myself that the six types of communication run throughout the entire program, and that each will always receive either major or minor emphasis, depending upon the developmental level of the child. If we look at the two modes of behavior, we have verbal and nonverbal. Included in the verbal mode are the usual oral, written, read, and heard. Early in the child's school career, I would place almost all emphasis upon the oral, spoken, and heard, moving to read and written only when the child has almost done it himself. This would apply across the board to all three types of behavior. Urgent attention, however, would be given to the nonverbal mode in all types of behavior at all points along the curriculum. The purpose of this progression is to allow the child to become increasingly proficient in the types of communication with which he is already familiar, assuming that more attention can be paid to the quality of his communication and his ability to interpret his world than if we force upon him a type of communication with which he has to struggle.

The foregoing illustrations give the general idea of the direction in which I would move in building a curriculum. To make the intent hopefully more clear, let me cite some specific classroom examples. Were I actually writing a curriculum for the use of teachers, I would describe such activities solely for the purpose of making clear the intent of the curriculum, not to prescribe what teachers must do with their own children.

Activities

First, classrooms would be characterized by talk, not silence, and the preponderance of such talk would be by children—among children and between children and the teacher. Where we now have reading groups, we would find discussion groups, painting groups, dance groups, drama groups, listening groups.

While there would be a professional teacher present, o adults would play a major role in the elementary school. better can discuss the language of the dance than someone wh in dance as a professional? Who better can help children to see what scientists are trying to say to the world than a scientist? Who better can explain the contribution of mathematics than the mathematician? Who better can help children understand the language of the fields than the scholars in the field? The role of the teacher becomes that of mediating for individual children and helping each child make personal use of what he has gleaned from the specialist.

Such activities require teachers who are skilled at ferreting out with each child the meaning of all such activities, teachers who honestly ask children questions which allow children to see for themselves what something means to them and for them. These are simple questions, which go something like this: What do you mean? Why does it mean that to you? How do you know? How do you feel about it? What difference does it make to you that you feel that way rather than another? What seems important to you? How do you think you come to know something? Why? Does this add to anything you already have found out? Does it make something clearer than it was before? Does it make you feel better about yourself? Do you now feel more comfortable about things than you did before you had the talk with the gentleman about matter and energy? Conversely, children will be asking similar questions of each other and of teachers.

As children acquire facility in communicating with spoken and heard language, they may work toward such facility with the written word—their own and that of others. The necessity for dialogue with other children, with the teacher, with other adults, and with materials does not decrease, however. For now children need to be asking of what they read the same questions teachers have been asking of children. The time at which this becomes appropriate will differ for each child. The determination is made on the basis of what is known about the child, not upon such an extraneous measure as how long he has been in school, nor upon some such astrological grounds as the number of years he has been alive or in what month he was born.

Other kinds of activities are relevant to other kinds of communication. As I have already mentioned, the performing arts offer children the opportunity to see themselves and what they have to say to the world in a light different from that shed upon them when they are limited to communicating with words. Creative dramatics gives a chance for "talking with" others in a unique way. And this talking lets others see an individual in a way he may not be able to demonstrate with verbal language alone. Sports of many types can be drawn upon in the same way and for the same reasons.

Evaluation

Evaluation techniques become more critical in the curriculum I have only hinted at than they have been in more traditional types of approaches. You will recall that I am using the term evaluation to mean a description of progress of an individual child toward specified objectives. The techniques are little different from the kinds of activities described earlier. Through questions and discussions, teachers will be collecting evidence to let them know whether children are becoming increasingly abler to cope with their world on and in their own terms.

Teachers will be able to tell whether and in what ways a child needs something in particular—stimulation, sympathy, a sensitive ear, a group opportunity, or solitude in which he may struggle with an idea with which he is involved. The core of the techniques to be employed is sensitive observation by teachers of individual children and thorough, comprehensive record keeping. It should be noted here that there is an important distinction to be made between and among evaluation, grading, and reporting. The latter two are based upon the first and therefore related to it. Yet grading and reporting are not synonymous with evaluation. In passing, if I were to have my way, regardless of the curriculum, I would abolish grading and improve techniques of evaluating and reporting.

The reason for stressing evaluation is that, in my judgment, we ought to be concerned with a child's progress, not with developing categories for him to fit or labels for him to wear. True evaluation is a learning experience for the child and is not judgmental. Nor is it used to threaten or cajole, or to elevate, or to make odious comparisons. It has as its purpose assisting each child to grow in whatever direction has been set by him or with him. It is to gather information with and about each child so that he may see himself in relation to goals of which he is at least aware.

Let me give just one simple illustration. Suppose that a physician were brought to a classroom to discuss his field with children. The teacher knows each child well. During the discussion she observes each child but in all likelihood with a different purpose for each child. She makes a careful record of the amount and nature of the interaction and communication. This information will be used in subsequent discussions with an individual child to chart his next moves. This, in my estimation, is evaluation.

In conclusion, certainly all the foregoing has implications for teaching and instruction, for school organization, for buildings, for nonprofessional personnel, for materials, for deployment of teachers and pupils. These, however, go much beyond the scope of this paper's purpose. It is important to note that these latter considerations follow, not precede, the establishment of a purpose of education and the curriculum.

It is also vital to keep constantly in mind that a curriculum as I have used the term is nothing more than a plan. It is also nothing less. For years in education we have traveled on the assumption that there is some relation between curriculum and instruction. Richard Hawthorne has developed a model which allows us to examine the extent and nature of this assumed relation; his study reveals that this relation is at best tenuous. Therefore, it is essential that we do not rely upon plans, no matter how well done, to make the changes so vitally needed in elementary education.

Many questions can be raised about the proposal I have made for the restructuring of the elementary curriculum. One of the most common reservations expressed about such new ventures is that children will not be prepared for any one of a number of things: junior high school, high school, college, or a vocation. My response has to be that that is not our problem. It is the problem of the junior high school, the high school, the college, the vocations. We might even influence education at these levels. Let us counter with the charge that these institutions have the shoe on the wrong foot; they are not prepared for individuals who are learning to live in the world.

My assignment for this paper was to construct a curriculum that is "way out" and to justify it. Whether or not I have succeeded is at best doubtful. Perhaps the task could have been carried out in four sentences: (a) The job of the elementary school is to start each child on the road to accepting himself and to coping successfully with the world in his own way and on his own terms. (b) The present program of the elementary school cannot do this job. (c) To construct a program that holds promise of allowing the elementary school to do the job, we must change the essence of the way we think and talk about the elementary school program, not simply try to make the same old things over into a new image.

Communication offers *one* possibility. (d) To build a new elementary curriculum which is relevant and real to the child requires untold intellectual and moral courage, as does any change in the face of opposition. However, given my position on the nature of man, I must make one last assertion: educators, being a part of humankind, are by nature courageous.

NEW CURRICULUM DESIGNS FOR CHILDREN

LOUISE M. BERMAN

In this article Louise Berman deals in a shortened form with the same topic she treats in her full-length book entitled, **New Priorities in the Curriculum.** Her curriculum focus on processes stems from her view that man is a "process-oriented being." In her book Berman states that "process-orientation characterizes persons who are able to handle themselves and the situations of which they are a part with adequacy and ease. Such persons are the contributors to as well as the recipients of society's resources. All educational institutions, particularly the school, should give high priority to fostering process concepts in to-day's children and youth, if personal adequacy and individual responsibility are among the major goals of school programs." *

---

* Louise M. Berman, *New Priorities in the Curriculum* (Columbus, Ohio: Charles E. Merrill Publishing Co., 1968), p. 10.

Given this point of view, it is easy to see why Berman focuses on humanistic processes—both affective and cognitive—rather than on the disciplines or any single process. The reader should compare her de-emphasis of the disciplines with those of Ammons (Chapter 10) and Wise (Chapter 7), for these authors share many points in common with her. With both Ammons and Wise, Berman shares the emphasis on process, and with Wise in particular, she shares an emphasis on the existential life of man.

In her treatment of the process of systematizing and forming attachments, Berman sets forth a strong position for a values (but not only a values) curriculum by building on the existentialists and the humanistic psychologists such as Buber, Rogers, and Maslow. Thus, it is via her emphasis on multiple processes that Berman is able to combine the affective with cognitive domain into a **humanistic processes** curriculum.

Whereas some educators have treated the affective domain and neglected the cognitive processes, or vice versa, Berman claims outright that these two aspects of man's nature cannot be treated separately. The reader must ask, of course, if the processes Berman designates are adequate and sufficient. Should these processes, such as systematizing and forming attachments, receive the top priority in a school's curriculum? In answering these questions the reader would do well to consider Berman's points in light of the articles by Ammons (Chapter 10), Wise (Chapter 7), and Mann (Chapter 9).

<hr />

A thorough treatment of the topic, "New Curriculum Designs for Children," lies beyond the space allotted for this paper. What

"New Curriculum Designs for Children" by Louise M. Berman is reprinted with permission from *The New Elementary School*, Alexander Frazier, ed., (Washington, D.C.: Association for Supervision and Curriculum Development, 1968), pp. 129–46. Reprinted with permission of the Association for Supervision and Curriculum Development and Louise M. Berman. Copyright © 1968 by the Association for Supervision and Curriculum Development. This selection is from pp. 129–31, 133–41.

can be done, however, is to present briefly some concepts and priorities that ought to be considered in developing curriculum designs both for today and for 25 years hence.

Design has a delightful connotation in that the root meaning is "to mark out." Inherent in the definition also is the concept of creating. If we are to mark out or create, certain materials are necessary. The designer, however, can arrange these as he sees fit. The pattern may be complex or simple, bold or subtle, subdued or vividly colored. . . .

BASIC ASSUMPTIONS REGARDING CURRICULUM DESIGNING

Now I would like to share with the reader certain beliefs on the nature of man and the nature of curriculum development that have helped shape my outlook and my proposals.

The Nature of Man

1. Man is a highly complex being. Oftentimes in thinking about him as we develop school programs, we have explained him in rather simple concepts. Such simplicity has caused untold damage in the planning of school programs, for man is seen in too unrealistic a manner.

2. Man is an ethical and aesthetic, a legal, social, psychological, and religious being. Any curricular design which fails to account for the many facets of man is cheating him of enhancement in critical areas.

3. We have also been erroneous in thinking about man as though his emotional and rational processes could be dealt with separately. We must strive for a set of concepts which does not dichotomize the person in this way.

4. We are on the fringe of possessing the tools to determine better how individuals learn. We are also on the edge of certain new developments in teaching styles. As knowl-

edge increases about learning and teaching, curriculum designs can be far more creative and imaginative.

The Nature of Curriculum Development

1. The language of the curriculum should derive its roots from the folklore of the people and the profession. Being a relatively new profession, we have adopted some pseudo-scientific terms which are not necessarily central to our tasks. Such use of language does not contribute to the integrity of the profession.

2. Automation and technological advances have caused us to give children more of the same in the curriculum rather than to develop unique curriculum designs which utilize the best of what we know about technological advances and human encounters.

3. The use of auxiliary personnel in the classroom is causing major shifts in who makes curricular decisions. The educational plaza and planned community concepts not only will bring more persons into the school but also will cause more overlap in the common experiences which children share with their parents. This may increase similarities between the experiences children have at home and at school.

4. Innovation for its own sake will die down. In its place will be more longitudinal studies.

5. Curriculum workers will be less enamored with the many analytic tools which have characterized much curriculum change within the past few years. New strides will be made in combining analytic with synthesizing skills so that comprehensive curriculum designs will emerge. More persons who can make a comprehensive design out of tangled skeins will be visible. Who knows—we may even see another John Dewey! . . .

NEW PRIORITIES IN THE CONTENT OF SCHOOL PROGRAMS

In the new elementary school, more care will be taken to select significant concepts to be taught than has been traditional in the past. The necessity to know about a staggering number of fields of knowledge will mean that educators will select only the most central ideas from key disciplines for inclusion in the elementary school program. We will not be concerned that all fields of study be included in elementary school programs. For example, we may have learned that the formal teaching of mathematics might better begin in upper elementary or junior high school.

In addition, much of the material treated in the elementary school will be chosen to help man better accommodate to and change the environment. The complexity of life will necessitate man's having at his disposal a set of tools that will enable him to maintain his own equilibrium in a world in which change rather than stability will be the order of the day.

Because curriculum workers will be more sophisticated in seeking to understand man, curriculum content will be selected with a view to developing or enhancing a particular view of the person. The discrepancy between behavioral objectives and what the school teaches will not be as great as it is now. To differentiate content from methodology and process may be difficult at the elementary level because much content will deal with basic human functions or processes such as becoming aware, forming attachments, creating, knowing, and so on.

Since the early 'sixties the schools have focused much of their attention upon scholarly knowing within the various disciplines. In the earlier stages of the curriculum reform movement, the study of the disciplines had well defined foci. Attention was given to the boundaries of the discipline, to relevant questions and modes of inquiry. Because much literature has been devoted to a consideration of the disciplines as the substance of the curriculum, there is no need to treat the topic in detail. The idea, during its inception, was a fruitful one. At the present time, however, some are questioning whether teachers are teaching the disciplines as modes of inquiry or whether their familiarity with the new materials is causing them to pass on the generalizations before children themselves have had the opportunity to discover or formulate them.[1]

Our hunch is that the new elementary school will continue to offer programs containing the recreated disciplines as they were originally conceived, but the study of such subjects will occupy only a portion of the day.

Let us now consider other areas which should receive top priority in the curriculum of the new elementary school.

New Emphases in the Communication Skills

Communication will be studied as a key to unlock our understanding of other persons who have lived before and those who are contemporaries. Less priority will be given in the elementary school to learning the formal properties of language.

One area that needs retooling is the field of the spoken word. Trends are evident at the secondary level which indicate new and needed emphases in speech. According to William Work, Executive Secretary of the Speech Association of America:

> Informative speaking, epitomized at its lowest level by the "What I Did Last Summer" speech and the book report, is getting less stress than is persuasive speaking. The latter develops the student's ability to analyze issues critically and competence to prepare

---

[1] This observation was made during a recent meeting of the Commission on Current Curriculum Developments of the Association for Supervision and Curriculum Development. For a view of one way of including the recreated disciplines in the curriculum, see: Alice Miel. "Knowledge and the Curriculum." In: *New Insights and the Curriculum*. Alexander Frazier, editor. Washington, D.C.: Association for Supervision and Curriculum Development, 1963. pp. 71–104.

suitable logical and emotional appeals for a specific audience that has been studied in depth.[2]

Since persons will have access to varieties of written materials, the elementary school as well as the secondary school will give increased attention to the persuasive components of speech. Good persuasive speaking involves logic that makes an impact. The mere reporting of factual data probably will be left to other forms of communication.

A second communication skill that will receive increased attention in school programs is that of nonverbal communication. Children will learn to be more discerning in their listening, picking up the subtle overtones as well as the gross, obvious points. They will learn to listen for hidden meanings as well as dictionary definitions of words. Children will learn to see telling gestures, facial expressions, characteristic modes of dress, and the utilization of space in professional and social settings.[3] In a world which is becoming increasingly smaller, the expectation cannot be that individuals will be able to communicate the spoken word effectively in the myriad of spoken and written languages. However, individuals will be expected to know something about the vital messages that people send through means other than words.

A third communication skill that will receive increased attention has been referred to by some as that of communion. Here we are concerned with interpersonal skills that enable a person to encounter another with authenticity and integrity. At the present time, a discussion of communion often implies lack of logic and scholarliness. Twenty-five years hence, hopefully we can teach this prime purpose of communication with knowledge and conviction.

---

[2] William Work. "New and Needed Developments in Speech." *NASSP Bulletin* 51(318):41; April 1967.

[3] For an examination of what the use of space may communicate, see: Edward T. Hall. *The Hidden Dimension.* New York: Doubleday & Company, Inc., 1966; readers may be acquainted with his earlier work, *The Silent Language.* New York: Doubleday & Company, Inc., 1959.

The Process of Systematizing

Traditionally much attention has been given to the teaching of the systems and orders which have been devised by others. Relatively little thought has been given to helping the child make sense of and systematize the world which he perceives. The existential world of the child will here be referred to as the internalized system.

In addition, the child needs to know the procedures that groups of persons use to make sense out of life in the wider community. These procedures are often more formalized and usually are external to the child. Both the informal and the formal, the internalized and externalized ways of making order should be part of the knowledge of the elementary school child.

INTERNALIZED ORDER. Writers, poets, religious leaders, dramatists, psychologists, and others who have been concerned with man's uniqueness have stressed the highly original ways in which each man takes in, reworks and organizes his experience. An analysis of the works of these experts in human nature can develop an awareness of the uniqueness of internalized ways of organizing or patterning. Such study helps us realize that no man can truly see or know the world of another which is so neatly hidden from human view. The meaning of individual modes of perceiving and organizing has been beautifully expressed by modern existentialists.[4]

One can infer also that writers concerned with individual modes of perceiving assume that perceptions are organized in accord with previous experiences, attitudes, dispositions, and values of the individual.[5] Some have referred to what happens between

---

[4] Among these are: Paul Tillich. *The Courage To Be.* New Haven, Connecticut: Yale University Press, 1952; Martin Buber. *I and Thou.* New York: Charles Scribner's Sons, 1958; second edition; Karl Jaspers. *Man in the Modern Age.* New York: Doubleday Anchor Books, 1957; and Michael Polanyi. *Personal Knowledge: Toward a Post-Critical Philosophy.* Chicago: University of Chicago Press, 1958.

[5] See: Arthur W. Combs and Donald Snygg. *Individual Behavior: A Perceptual Approach to Behavior.* New York: Harper and Brothers, 1959; revised

the time that perception occurs and behavior and thinking are noted as ego processing.[6]

In any event, the highly personal world of each student will be prized. How to derive, maintain, and change the frameworks which help an individual tie his experiences, feelings, and information together will be given high priority in new school programs. At the present time, our knowledge is scant about how to provide such learning opportunities. Soon, however, children will become aware of the remarkable facility which they possess and will learn to strengthen it.

Some concepts that can and ought to be taught about the process of internalized ordering are the following:

1. Each person takes in, uses and makes use of his perceptions in unique ways.

2. The uniqueness of individual perceiving and ordering of impressions is a peculiarly human function. Each individual should prize his own modes of organizing and also the right of others to do the same.

3. Personalized frameworks vary in their degree of stability. At times persons may wish to reevaluate their organizational schemes in order to accommodate new ideas which do not fit old patterns. In other words, a pattern helps an individual order his thoughts but should not be so inviolable that it governs his total intake of ideas.

4. The verbalizing and comparing of children's modes of organizing help each sharpen his framework and change when such action seems appropriate.

---

edition; also *Perceiving, Behaving, Becoming: A New Focus for Education.* Arthur W. Combs, editor. Washington, D.C.: Association for Supervision and Curriculum Development, 1962.

[6] See: Eli M. Bower. "Personality and Individual Social Maladjustment." In: *Social Deviancy among Youth.* Sixty-fifth Yearbook of the National Society for the Study of Education, Part I, Chicago: University of Chicago Press, 1966. pp. 103–34; also William G. Hollister. "Preparing the Minds of the Future: Enhancing Ego Processes Through Curriculum Development." In: *Curriculum Change: Direction and Process.* Robert R. Leeper, editor. Washington, D.C.: Association for Supervision and Curriculum Development, 1966. pp. 27–42.

5. A variety of emotional states may accompany the process of organizing. When stability is present, the child may feel contented and satisfied. Dissatisfaction and feelings of frustration may accompany an attempt at reorganization.

6. Individuals should strive for beauty, integrity, and a sense of priority in the development of internalized frameworks.

EXTERNALIZED ORDER. Were each individual to live on a desert island alone, there would be no need for external order. Because, however, persons must live together in groups of various types, each group having different expectations, it is necessary that ways be found to maintain external order. Many sources of externally derived and imposed order could be described, but for our purposes, only one will be considered. It is chosen because it has not been given much attention in developing programs for elementary school children.

Possessing much potential for helping persons in groups prevent and resolve conflicts and having the qualities to enable the establishment of order, the law is an area from which we can derive many insights to forward our concepts of order. Harold Berman and William Greiner say:

> Law is an institution in the sense of an integrated pattern or process of social behavior and ideas. What goes on inside courts, legislatures, law offices, and other places in which law-making, law-enforcing, law-administering, and law-interpreting are carried on, together with what goes on inside the minds of people thinking with reference to what goes on in those places, forms a law way of acting and thinking, which overlaps but is not identical with economic, religious, political, and other social ways of acting and thinking. [Italics removed.]

> As soon as law is defined in terms of a set of actions and ideas, instead of in terms of a set of rules, it becomes possible to study its interrelationships with other types of patterned behavior and thought.[7]

---

[7] Harold Berman and William R. Greiner. *The Nature and Functions of Law*. Brooklyn, New York: The Foundation Press, Inc., 1966. pp. 6–7.

According to these authors, law enables the study of the formal institutional processes by which social order is achieved. This is coupled with a theoretical framework for explaining and justifying the more formal processes.[8]

They later say:

> Law is thus seen as a special kind of ordering process, a special type of process of restoring, maintaining or creating social order—a type of ordering which is primarily neither the way of friendship nor the way of force but something in between.[9]

Law has a certain formality about it. It differs from many agreements and contracts made among persons in that it is deliberate and definite. Its main functions are:

> (a) To resolve disputes, (b) to facilitate and protect voluntary arrangements, (c) to mold and remold the moral and legal conceptions of a society, and (d) in the Western tradition, at least, to maintain historical continuity and consistency of doctrine.[10]

If insights from the discipline of law are to influence externally imposed organizing systems, then students must learn to deal with conflict, dispute, and alternatives within the school curriculum. Controversy, competing ideologies, and passion often characterize real-life situations, yet we often teach as though critical thinking takes place in a neutral, dispassionate environment. Thus, the following ideas are among those that will be taught concerning the external ordering of ideas or events:

1. Formal, deliberate attempts at ordering are necessary for the maintenance of any group.
2. Procedures are attempts at ordering and are ways of resolving problems when a group works together.

----

[8] *Ibid.,* p. 12.
[9] *Ibid.,* p. 28.
[10] *Ibid.,* p. 36.

3. Greater emphasis upon the analysis of public issues helps individuals see the prerequisites to the analysis of conflict in addition to the use of critical thinking skills.[11]

4. Much of our knowledge which appears to be private has within it many tacit components which have been derived from our public participation in human affairs. Children need to bring to the level of awareness the various sources of their knowing and ordering.[12]

Man by nature seeks to systematize his experience. Existentialist thinkers have helped us see the fact that each man orders his experience in a different way. Social orders, such as law, point out the formal and external arrangements that must be made among persons if adequate group functioning is to take place.

The young child is constantly concerned about procedures governing his play with his peers. We deprive the child by not letting him in on some of the formal procedures for peacemaking and the resolution of conflict. The child is also interested in his own uniqueness. We do him an injustice by not helping him better understand the internalized processes he can develop to make sense out of what happens to him.

The Nature of Attachments

As life in the next few years continues to move ahead at an ever-increasing rate, persons will have the opportunity to form attachments to a wider variety of persons, objects, or ideas. Those things to which a person ought to become attached, as prescribed by cultural norms, will not become as clearly delimited as they are today. For example, a re-examination of the interests, roles, and

---

[11] See: Donald W. Oliver and James P. Shaver. *Teaching Public Issues in the High School*. Boston: Houghton Mifflin Company, 1966. Although written for secondary school educators, the book has many implications for the elementary school.

[12] See: Michael Polanyi. *The Tacit Dimension*. New York: Doubleday & Company, Inc., 1966.

attitudes commonly ascribed to each sex will probably broaden the scope of what are appropriate sex roles in tomorrow's society.

Throughout different stages in life, individuals may form different types of attachments. For example, mutually satisfying relationships that a child often forms with adults represent a necessary kind of attachment if the child is to possess the emotional stamina to carry on many of life's challenges in his later years. Bensman and Rosenberg say, "Unconditional love, warmth, affection, intimate care, and attention are literally priceless; their absence inflicts overwhelming and irremediable damage." [13] The person who has not found appropriate ways of relating to others may find himself in the position of subconsciously seeking the attention of others to the neglect of other types of constructive work or play.

Even as the child particularly needs the sustaining support of other persons, he must also define how he will relate to society in order to accomplish what he perceives to be useful ends. Bensman and Rosenberg say:

> It follows that the potentially creative human being must "use" society to extract from it all the support it has to offer while mustering his resources to repel available "solutions" manufactured for him as well as attractive or oppressive alernatives to his own natural unfolding. All this implies that one needs to develop in childhood the psychological strength to define his own tasks, to create his own vision and not to let himself be deflected from it. [Italics removed.] [14]

As an individual matures, creates his own vision, and defines his tasks, he determines that to which he will devote time, energy, and resources. The nature of his commitments determines his friends and those persons to whom he shows love and affection. The degree to which he gains a response from that to which he attaches himself

---

[13] Joseph Bensman and Bernard Rosenberg. "Healthy Potentialities and the Healthy Society." In: *Explorations of Human Potentialities.* Herbert A. Otto, editor. Springfield, Illinois: Charles C Thomas, Publisher, 1966. p. 214.

[14] *Ibid.,* p. 25.

to a great extent determines how he nourishes what has the potential to become dear to him.

The elementary school program must make provision for children to become aware of their commitments and possibly to change them. Some children may have a strong orientation to persons, either family or friends or both. Others may prefer to deal with objects or ideas.

An understanding of attachments enables the child to understand better the nature of love and its relationship to sex, materialism, idealism, religion, and other factors and causes which absorb men's energies. Only as the child learns that attachments cannot be made to many objects or things simultaneously will he learn to differentiate the good from the better and the better from the best. He will learn to detach himself at times from certain objects and persons in order to attach himself to what, in his best judgment, should receive the totality of his energies, thought, and devotion at a particular moment in time.

Other Priorities in Content

Limitations of space preclude our going into detail concerning other areas which will be given increased attention in the school of the future, but let me mention a few vital topics.

BALANCE BETWEEN SPONTANEITY AND THE CULTURAL CONSERVE. "The arch catalyzer of creativity is spontaneity, by definition from the Latin *sua sponte* which means 'coming from within.' " [15] Spontaneity operates in the present and is a new response to an old situation or an adequate response to a new situation. The finished product is the cultural conserve that preserves the values of a culture. In addition it plays a significant role as a *"springboard for enticing new spontaneity toward creativity."* [16] Children, particu-

---

[15] J. L. Moreno. "Spontaneity, Creativity, and Human Potentialities." In: Herbert A. Otto, *op. cit.,* p. 46.

[16] *Ibid,* p. 47.

larly in the middle grades, will learn to differentiate more sharply between spontaneity which takes place as a result of knowledge of a subject or area and spontaneity which comes about in an undisciplined way. More emphasis will be placed upon disciplined forms of inquiry so that creativity can frequently be intentional.[17]

PREPARATION FOR DIFFERENT STAGES OF LIFE. We are living in a youth-oriented culture, and today's children are taught in subtle ways to be intolerant of old age. Tomorrow's school will focus upon the contributions persons make in the various stages of life. The transiency of life will be stressed; the topic of death will not be unfamiliar in school programs. There is research to support the concept that persons who have learned to function at high creative levels have overcome major physical handicaps in the attempt to utilize their potential as long as possible.[18] Schools, therefore, will give increased attention to developing skills that will give satisfaction during both youth and old age.

WONDER AS AN INGREDIENT TO PERSONAL KNOWING. The new elementary school curriculum will make available opportunities to wonder. Students will learn to identify their own sources of curiosity, and the topic will be considered within school subjects as appropriate. When a school subject becomes so crystallized that the capacity to wonder is no longer fostered by its teaching, then new modes of looking at the subject will be ascertained.[19]

INTERNAL AWARENESS. Unless an individual is aware of the multiplicity of factors which the school brings to bear upon him, a given task may not produce the intended outcome. Thus, children

---

[17] See: John I. Goodlad and others. *The Changing School Curriculum.* New York: The Fund for the Advancement of Education, 1966. p. 91, for a discussion of the concept of "disciplined discovery."

[18] See Leonard Pearson. "Aging Phenomena in the Perspective of Human Potential." In: Herbert A. Otto, *op. cit.,* pp. 112–34.

[19] For a consideration of the lack of attention to wonder in the new mathematics programs, see: Brother L. Raphael. "The Return of the Old Mathematics." *The Mathematics Teacher* 60: 14–17; January 1967.

should early become aware of their modes of thinking, of the assumptions underlying their values, and of their prevailing ways of behaving. How to become aware of one's self will be among the content that is taught in the school.

PART III

SELECTED BIBLIOGRAPHY

ALBERTY, HAROLD, "A Proposal for Reorganizing the High-School Curriculum on the Basis of a Core Program." *Progressive Education* 28 (November, 1950): 57–61.

ALBERTY, HAROLD, "Designing Programs to Meet the Common Needs of Youth," in *Adapting the Secondary-School Program to the Needs of Youth,* ed. Nelson B. Henry. Fifty-second Yearbook, Part I of the National Society for the Study of Education. Chicago: University of Chicago Press, 1953. Pp. 118–40.

ALBERTY, HAROLD, "Should the Modern Secondary-School Curriculum Be Experience Centered?" *The Bulletin of the National Association of Secondary-School Principals* 33 (April, 1949): 115–24.

219

ALBERTY, HAROLD B. and ELSIE J., *Reorganizing the High School Curriculum,* 3rd ed. New York: The Macmillan Company, 1962.

AMMONS, MARGARET, "Communication: A Curriculum Focus," in *A Curriculum for Children,* ed. Alexander Frazier. Washington, D.C.: Association for Supervision and Curriculum Development, 1969.

BELLACK, ARNO A., "What Knowledge Is of Most Worth?" *The High School Journal* 48 (February, 1965): 318–32.

BERMAN, LOUISE M., *New Priorities in the Curriculum.* Columbus, Ohio: Charles E. Merrill Publishing Co., 1968.

BERMAN, LOUISE M., "New Curriculum Designs for Children," in *The New Elementary School,* ed. Alexander Frazier. Washington, D.C.: Association for Supervision and Curriculum Development, 1968.

BOBBITT, FRANKLIN, *The Curriculum.* Boston: Houghton Mifflin Company, 1918.

BOBBITT, FRANKLIN, *How to Make a Curriculum.* Boston: Houghton Mifflin Company, 1924.

BORTON, TERRY, *Reach, Touch and Teach.* New York: McGraw-Hill Book Company, 1970.

BOWERS, C. A., "Existentialism and Educational Theory." *Educational Theory* 15 (July, 1965): 222–29.

BROWN, GEORGE, *Human Teaching for Human Learning.* New York: The Viking Press, Inc., 1971.

BRUNER, JEROME S., *The Process of Education.* Cambridge, Mass.: Harvard University Press, 1960.

BUETHE, CHRIS, "A Curriculum of Value." *Educational Leadership* 26 (October, 1968), 31–33.

CASWELL, HOLLIS L., "Developing Social Understanding in the Elementary School." *Elementary School Journal* 36 (January, 1936): 341–43.

CHARTERS, W. W., "Educational Aims, Ideals, and Activities." *Journal of Educational Research* 3 (May, 1921): 322–25.

CLOUSER, LUCY WELLER and MILLIKAN, CHLOE ETHEL, *Kindergarten-Primary Activities Based on Community Life.* New York: The Macmillan Company, 1929.

COMBS, ARTHUR W., ed., *Perceiving, Behaving and Becoming.* Washington, D.C.: Association for Supervision and Curriculum Development, 1962.

CRARY, RYLAND W., *Humanizing the School*. New York: Alfred A. Knopf, Inc., 1969.

DEWEY, JOHN, *The Child and the Curriculum*. Chicago: University of Chicago Press, 1902.

DEWEY, JOHN, *Democracy and Education*. New York: The Macmillan Company, 1916.

DEWEY, JOHN, *Experience and Education*. New York: The Macmillan Company, 1938.

DEWEY, JOHN, *How We Think: A Restatement of the Relation of Reflective Thinking to the Educative Process*. Boston: D. C. Heath & Company, 1933.

DEWEY, JOHN, "My Pedagogic Creed." *The School Journal* 54 (January, 1897): 77–80.

DEWEY, JOHN, *The School and Society*. Chicago: University of Chicago Press, 1899.

DEWEY, JOHN, "The Theory of the Chicago Experiment," in Katherine Camp Mayhew and Anna Camp Edwards, *The Dewey School*. New York, Appleton-Century-Crofts, 1936.

DREWS, ELIZABETH MONROE, "Self-Actualization: A New Focus for Education." *Learning and Mental Health in the School*. 1966 Yearbook, Association for Supervision and Curriculum Development, ed. Walter B. Waetjen and Robert R. Leeper. Washington, D.C.: Association for Supervision and Curriculum Development, 1966.

EDUCATIONAL POLICIES COMMISSION, *Education for All American Youth: A Further Look*. Washington, D.C.: National Education Association, 1952.

FEATHERSTONE, WILLIAM B., *A Functional Curriculum for Youth*. New York: American Book Company, 1950.

FEATHERSTONE, W. B., "The Place of Subjects in an Integrated Curriculum." *California Quarterly of Secondary Education* 9 (April, 1935): 235–46.

FENNER, JAMES J., "Reconnection for Relevance: A Proposed New High School Curriculum." *Teachers College Record* 71 (February, 1970): 423–38.

FIRTH, GERALD R., "Youth Education: A Curricular Perspective." *Youth Education: Problems/Perspectives/Promises*, ed. Raymond H. Muessig. 1968 Yearbook of the Association for Supervision and Curriculum Development. Washington, D.C.: Association for Supervision and Curriculum Development, 1968.

FREDERICK, O. I. and FARQUEAR, L. J., "Areas of Human Activity." *Journal of Educational Research* 30 (May, 1937): 672–79.

FREEMAN, FRANK N., "An Analysis of the Basis of the Activity Curriculum." *Elementary School Journal* 35 (May, 1935): 655–61.

FRIEDMAN, NORMAN, "The American School: Guild or Factory," *Teachers College Record,* 70 (May, 1969): 697–713.

GILES, H. H., McCUTCHEN, S. P., and ZECHIEL, A. N., *Exploring the Curriculum*. New York: Harper & Row, Publishers, 1942.

HAND, HAROLD C., "The Case for the Common Learnings Course." *Science Education* 32 (February, 1948): 5–11.

HANNA, LAVONNE A., "Proposals for the Secondary School Curriculum." *Progressive Education* 28 (November, 1950): 62–67.

HEMMING, JAMES, *Teach Them to Live*. 2d ed. London: Longmans, Green and Co. Ltd., 1957.

HIRST, PAUL H., "Liberal Education and the Nature of Knowledge." *Philosophical Analysis and Education,* ed. Reginald D. Archambault. New York: The Humanities Press, Inc., 1965.

HOPKINS, L. THOMAS, "Arguments Favoring Integration." *Teachers College Record* 36 (April, 1935): 604–12.

HOPKINS, L. THOMAS, "Curriculum Development." *Teachers College Record* 37 (February, 1936): 441–47.

HOPKINS, L. THOMAS, "Needs and Interests: A Sufficient Basis for the Elementary School Curriculum." *Viewpoints on Educational Issues and Problems*. Thirty-ninth Annual Schoolmen's Week Proceedings. Philadelphia: University of Pennsylvania, 1952.

HUEBNER, DWAYNE, ed., *A Reassessment of the Curriculum*. New York: Bureau of Publications, Teachers College, Columbia University, 1964.

HULLFISH, H. GORDON, "Reflective Thinking as Educational Method." *Problems of Educational Freedom*. Bloomington: Bulletin of the School of Education, Indiana University, 37 (March, 1961): 1–12.

HULLFISH, H. GORDON and SMITH, PHILIP G., *Reflective Thinking: The Method of Education*. New York: Dodd, Mead and Co., 1961.

JENNINGS, HELEN HALL, "Sociodrama as Educative Process." *Fostering Mental Health in Our Schools.* 1950 Yearbook of the Association for Supervision and Curriculum Development. Washington, D.C.: Association for Supervision and Curriculum Development, 1950.

JERSILD, ARTHUR T., *Child Development and the Curriculum.* New York: Bureau of Publications, Teachers College, Columbia University, 1946.

JOINT COMMITTEE ON CURRICULUM, HENRY HARAP, Chairman, *The Changing Curriculum.* New York, Appleton-Century-Crofts, 1937.

JUDD, CHARLES H., "Curriculum in View of the Demands on the Schools." *School Review* 49 (January, 1934): 20–25.

KELLEY, EARL C., *In Defense of Youth.* Englewood Cliffs, N.J.: Prentice-Hall, Inc., 1962.

KILPATRICK, WILLIAM HEARD, "The Essentials of the Activity Movement," *Progressive Education* 11 (October, 1934): 346–59.

KILPATRICK, WILLIAM HEARD, *Foundations of Method.* New York: The Macmillan Company, 1926.

KILPATRICK, WILLIAM HEARD, "The Project Method." *Teachers College Record* 19 (September, 1918): 319–35.

KILPATRICK, WILLIAM HEARD, *Remaking the Curriculum.* New York: Newson and Co., 1936.

KING, ARTHUR R., JR. and BROWNELL, JOHN A., *The Curriculum and the Disciplines of Knowledge: A Theory of Curriculum Practice.* New York: John Wiley & Sons, Inc., 1966.

LACK, CLARENCE A., "Love as a Basis for Organizing Curriculum." *Educational Leadership* 26 (April, 1969): 693–701.

LANE, ROBERT HILL, *The Progressive Elementary School.* Boston: Houghton Mifflin Company, 1938.

MACDONALD, JAMES B., "The High School in Human Terms: Curriculum Design." *Humanizing the Secondary School,* ed. Norman K. Hamilton and J. Galen Saylor. Washington: D.C., Association for Supervision and Curriculum Development, 1969.

MACDONALD, JAMES B., "The Person in the Curriculum." *Precedents and Promise,* ed. Helen F. Robison. New York: Teachers College Press, Columbia University, 1966.

224   Selected Bibliography

MACDONALD, JAMES B., "The 'Why' of Core: A Rationale for Teaching-Learning." *Core Curriculum: The Why and the What*, ed. Rolland Callaway. Milwaukee: University of Wisconsin-Milwaukee, 1966.

MANN, JOHN S., "High School Student Protest and the New Curriculum Worker: A Radical Alliance." *A New Look at Progressive Education*. 1972 Yearbook, Association for Supervision and Curriculum Development, ed. James R. Squire. Washington, D.C.: Association for Supervision and Curriculum Development, 1972.

MERIAM, JUNIUS L., "A Life Activity Curriculum." *Teachers College Record* 33 (October, 1931): 15–25.

METCALF, LAWRENCE E., and HUNT, MAURICE P., "Relevance and the Curriculum." *Phi Delta Kappan*, 51 (March, 1970): 358–61.

MITCHELL, LUCY SPRAGUE, *Our Children and Our Schools*. New York: Simon & Schuster, Inc., 1950.

MOSSMAN, LOIS COFFEY, *The Activity Concept: An Interpretation*. New York: The Macmillan Company, 1940.

National Society for the Study of Education. *The Activity Movement*. Thirty-third Yearbook, Part II. Bloomington, Ill.: Public School Publishing Co., 1934.

National Society for the Study of Education, *The Integration of Educational Experiences*. Fifty-seventh Yearbook, Part III. Chicago: University of Chicago Press, 1958.

PHENIX, PHILIP H., "The Disciplines as Curriculum Content." *Curriculum Crossroads*, ed. A. Harry Passow. New York: Bureau of Publications, Teachers College, Columbia University, 1962.

PHENIX, PHILIP H., "The Moral Imperative in Contemporary American Education." *Perspectives on Education* 2 (Winter, 1969): 6–13.

PHENIX, PHILIP H., *Realms of Meaning: A Philosophy of the Curriculum for General Education*. New York: McGraw-Hill Book Company, 1964.

Phi Delta Kappan 51, No. 7 (March, 1970). Issue theme is "Curriculum for the 70's."

RATHS, LOUIS E., HARMIN, MERRILL, and SIMON, SIDNEY B., *Values and Teaching*. Columbus, Ohio: Charles E. Merrill Publishing Co., 1966.

RAUP, R. BRUCE, AXTELLE, GEORGE E.; BENNE, KENNETH B.; and SMITH, B. OTHANEL, *The Improvement of Practical Intelligence: The Central*

Task of Education. New York: Bureau of Publications, Teachers College, Columbia University, 1943.

Report of the Harvard Committee, *General Education in a Free Society.* Cambridge, Mass.: Harvard University Press, 1945.

RUBIN, LOUIS J. ed., *Life Skills in School and Society.* 1969 Yearbook of the Association for Supervision and Curriculum Development. Washington, D.C.: Association for Supervision and Curriculum Development, 1969.

RUGG, HAROLD, *Culture and Education in America.* New York: Harcourt Brace Jovanovich, Inc., 1931.

RUGG, HAROLD and SHUMAKER, ANN, *The Child-Centered School: An Appraisal of the New Education.* Yonkers-on-Hudson, New York: World Book Company, 1928.

SCHOENCHEN, GUSTAV G., *The Activity School.* New York: Longmans, Green and Co. Ltd., 1940.

STRATEMEYER, FLORENCE B.; FORKNER, HAMDEN L.; McKIM, MARGARET G.; PASSOW, A. HARRY, *Developing a Curriculum for Modern Living.* New York: Bureau of Publications, Teachers College, Columbia University, 1947. Second Edition, 1957.

STRUTHERS, ALICE BALL, "Integration—Some Underlying Principles and Implications." *California Quarterly of Secondary Education* 9 (October, 1933): 13–18.

UMSTAUD, J. G., "Integration as an Educational Concept." *High School Journal,* 23 (October, 1940): 265–70.

Washburne, John N., "Why an Activity Program?" *School and Society* 39 (June 16, 1934): 784.

WEEKS, RUTH MARY, Chairman, *A Correlated Curriculum.* A Report of the Committee on Correlation of the National Council of Teachers of English. New York: Appleton-Century-Crofts, 1936.

WEINBERG, ALVIN M., "But Is the Teacher Also a Citizen?" *Science* 149 (August 6, 1965): 601–6.

WEINSTEIN, GERALD and FANTINI, MARIO D., eds. *Toward Humanistic Education: A Curriculum of Affect.* New York: Praeger Publishers, Inc., 1970.

WISE, GENE, "Integrative Education for a Dis-integrated World." *Teachers College Record* 67 (March, 1966): 391–401.